Praise for Swami Vivekananda

"I have come here (Belur Math) to pay my homage and respect to the revered memory of Swami Vivekananda, whose birthday is being celebrated today. I have gone through his works very thoroughly, and after having gone through them, the love that I had for my country became a thousand-fold."

—*Mahatma Gandhi*

"The going forth of Vivekananda as the heroic soul destined to take the world between his two hands and change it was the first visible sign that India was awake . . . He was a power if ever there was one, a very lion among men. We perceive his influence still working gigantically in something grand, intuitive, upheaving . . ."

—*Sri Aurobindo*

"Please send me the book by Swami Vivekananda. It is more than a pleasure, it is a broadening of the soul."

—*Leo Tolstoy*

"The paragon of all Unity systems is the Vedanta philosophy of India, and the paragon of Vedantist missionaries was the late Swami Vivekananda who visited our land some years ago. I have just been reading some of Vivekananda's addresses in England, which I had not seen. The man is simply a wonder for oratorical power . . . the Swami is an honor to humanity."

—*William James*
"Father of American Psychology"

"Where can you find a man like him? Study what he wrote, and learn from his teachings, for if you do, you will gain immense strength. Take advantage of the fountain of wisdom, of Spirit, and of fire that flowed through Vivekananda!"

—*Jawaharlal Nehru*
First Prime Minister of India

"Vivekananda said that there was the power of God in every man, that God wanted to have our service through the poor. This is what I call real gospel. This gospel showed the path of infinite freedom from man's tiny egocentric self beyond the limits of all selfishness. This was no sermon relating to a particular ritual, nor was it a narrow injunction to be imposed upon one's external life. Vivekananda's gospel marked the awakening of man in his fullness . . . If you want to know India, study Vivekananda."

—*Rabindranath Tagore*

"I cannot write about Vivekananda without going into raptures. Reckless in his sacrifice, unceasing in his activity, boundless in his love, profound and versatile in his wisdom, exuberant in his emotions, Swamiji was a full-blooded masculine personality and a fighter to the core of his being. I can go on for hours and yet fail to do the slightest justice to that great man. He was so great, so profound, so complex. He was a Yogi of the highest spiritual level, in direct communion with the Truth, who consecrated his whole life to the moral and spiritual uplift of his nation and of humanity."

—*Subhas Chandra Bose*

"Swami Vivekananda will be remembered as one of the most significant figures in the whole history of Indian religion, comparable in importance to such great teachers as Shankara and Ramanuja. Since the days of the Indian missionaries who traveled in Southeast Asia and China preaching Buddhism and Hinduism more than a thousand years earlier, he was the first Indian religious teacher to make an impression outside India."

—*A. L. Basham*

"Vivekananda's words are great music, phrases in the style of Beethoven, stirring rhythms like the march of Handel choruses. I cannot touch these sayings of his at thirty years distance without receiving a thrill through my body like an electric shock. The present leaders of India: Gandhi, Aurobindo, and Tagore, have grown, flowered, and borne fruit under the double constellation of the Swan (Ramakrishna) and the Eagle (Vivekananda) — a fact publicly acknowledged by both Gandhi and Aurobindo."

—*Romain Rolland*

PATHWAYS
to JOY

PATHWAYS
to JOY

THE MASTER VIVEKANANDA

On the Four Yoga Paths to God

Edited by
DAVE DELUCA

NEW WORLD LIBRARY
NOVATO, CALIFORNIA

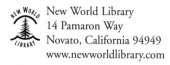 New World Library
14 Pamaron Way
Novato, California 94949
www.newworldlibrary.com

Cover design by Antista Fairclough
Book design by Madonna Gauding

PUBLISHER CATALOGING-IN-PUBLICATION DATA

Pathways to joy / edited by Dave DeLuca.
p. ; cm.
ISBN 978-1-930722-67-5 (pbk.)
A selection of 108 sacred teachings of Swami Vivekananda,
who brought yoga and the ancient wisdom of Vedanta philosophy
to the West at the 1893 Parliament of Religions.
Includes bibliographical references.
1. Vivekananda, Swami, 1863-1902. 2. Yoga. 3. Philosophy,
Hindu. 4. Religious life — Hinduism.
I. DeLuca, Dave.
BL1280.292.V58 P38 2006
294.5/55 — dc22 0606

ISBN 978-1-930722-67-5 (pbk.)
Printed in the United States of America

 New World Library is a proud memeber of the Green Press Initiative.

10 9 8 7 6 5 4 3 2

Dedicated to my mother, Annette DeLuca,
in honor of a lifetime of kindness,
service, and selfless love

Contents

Classical Yoga

———•◆•———

Jnana Yoga

———•◆•———

Karma Yoga

Bhakti Yoga

Raja Yoga

———•◆•———

Appendix

Acknowledgments

My deepest thanks to the following:

Swami Swahananda, for his majestic kindness and encouragement, and for his generous blessings in the compiling and editing of Swamiji's lectures and writings.

Swami Sarvadevananda, for his unwavering support, and for his continually inspiring example of goodness and spiritual light.

Shiva, for his invaluable assistance, and for his consistent and heartfelt enthusiasm during this long period of compiling and editing.

Swami Nikhilananda, for his editions of Vivekananda's works, and for his wonderful biography of Swamiji. These books first exposed me to Swami Vivekananda, and they have been great sources of inspiration for many years.

Huston Smith, for his inspiring example of universalism, so beautifully displayed in his great work *The World's Religions,* the book that first pointed me toward Hinduism, Vedanta, and Swami Vivekananda.

Pravrajika Vrajaprana, for her powerful and ongoing support.

All of the wonderful people of the Vedanta Society of Southern California, who have encouraged my efforts to bring Swami Vivekananda and his work to the attention of the American public.

The Advaita Ashrama, Calcutta, for permission to reprint material from the following books: *The Complete Works of Swami Vivekananda; The Life of Swami Vivekananda; Vivekananda: A Biography in Pictures;* and *Swami Vivekananda in the West: New Discoveries.*

Swami Vivekananda's writings need no introduction from anybody. They make their own irresistible appeal.

— *Mahatma Gandhi*

Swami Vivekananda, the Hindu monk, spoke three times in Des Moines. During his stay in the city Vivekananda met many of the best people in the city, who found their time well spent discussing religious and metaphysical questions with him. But it was woe to the man who undertook to combat the monk on his own ground. His replies came like flashes of lightning, and the venturesome questioner was sure to be impaled on the Indian's shining intellectual lance. The workings of his mind, so subtle and so brilliant, so well stored and so well trained, dazzled his hearers, but it was always a most interesting study. He said nothing unkind, for his nature would not permit that. Those who came to know him best found him the most gentle and lovable of men, so honest, frank, and unpretending, always grateful for the many kindnesses that were shown him. Vivekananda and his cause found a place in the hearts of all true Christians.

—Iowa State Register, *December 3, 1893*

Oneness

The Ancient Wisdom of Vedanta

VIVEKANANDA AS AN ITINERANT MONK, BELGAUM, INDIA,

The Vedanta Philosophy

I CAME HERE TO REPRESENT a philosophy from India that is called the Vedanta philosophy. This philosophy is very, very ancient; it is the outcome of that mass of ancient Aryan literature known by the name of the Vedas. It is, as it were, the very flower of all the speculations and experiences and analyses embodied in that mass of literature collected and culled through centuries. This Vedanta philosophy has certain peculiarities. In the first place, it is perfectly impersonal: it does not owe its origin to any person or prophet, and it does not build itself around one person as a center. Yet it has nothing to say against philosophies that do build themselves around certain persons. In later days in India, other philosophies and systems arose, built around certain persons — such as Buddhism or many of our present sects. They each have a certain leader to whom they owe allegiance, just as the Christians and Muslims have. But the Vedanta philosophy stands at the background of all these various sects, and there is no fight and no antagonism between the Vedanta and any other system in the world.

Vedanta claims that the human soul is divine, and that all this that we see around us is the outcome of that consciousness of the divine. Everything that is strong and good and powerful in human nature is the outpouring of that divinity, and though only potential in many, there is no difference between one human being and another essentially, all being alike divine. There is, as it were, an infinite ocean behind, and you and I are like so many waves coming out of that infinite ocean; and each one of us is trying our best to manifest that infinite outside. Each one of us has that infinite ocean of Existence, Knowledge, and Bliss as our birthright, our real nature; and the difference between us is caused by the greater or lesser power to manifest that divinity. Therefore, the Vedanta teaches that each of us should be treated not as what we manifest, but as what we stand for. Each human being stands for the divine, and therefore, each one of us should be helpful, not by condemning others, but by helping others to call forth the divinity that is within them.

Vedanta has no quarrel with those who do not yet understand this divinity of the soul. Consciously or unconsciously, every human being is trying to unfold that divinity. Each of us is like an infinite spring, coiled up in a small box, and that spring is trying to unfold itself; and all the social phenomena that we see is the result of this trying to unfold.

Now, this idea of the divinity of the soul, claims the Vedanta, is to be found in all religions, whether in India or outside of it; only, in some of them, the idea is expressed through mythology, and in others, through symbology. The Vedanta claims that all that we call ethics and morality and doing good to others is but the manifestation of this oneness. There are moments when each of us feels that we are one with the universe, and we rush forth to express it, whether we know it or not. This expression of oneness is what we call love and sympathy, and it is the basis of all our ethics and morality. It is summed up in the Vedanta philosophy by the celebrated aphorism *Tat Twam Asi*, "Thou art That."

To every person, this is taught: Thou art one with this Universal Being, and, as such, every soul that exists is your soul; and every body that exists is your body; and in hurting anyone, you hurt yourself, in loving anyone, you love yourself. As soon as a current of hatred is thrown outside, whomsoever else it hurts, it also hurts you; and if love comes out from you, it is bound to come back to you.

You are the Infinite, only you are not conscious of it now; but you are struggling to reach this consciousness of the Infinite, and perfection will be reached when full consciousness of this Infinite comes.

Another peculiar idea of the Vedanta is that because the goal is the same, we must allow this infinite variation in religious thought, and not try to bring everybody to the same opinion. As the Vedantist says in his poetical language, "As so many rivers, having their source in different mountains, roll down, and at last come into the sea — so, all these various creeds and religions, taking their start from different standpoints and running through crooked or straight courses, at last come unto Thee."

This is one of the great lessons that the Vedanta has to teach. Knowing that consciously or unconsciously we are struggling to reach the same goal, why should we be impatient? If one man is slower than another, we need not be impatient, and we need not curse or revile him. When our eyes are opened and our hearts are purified, the work of the same divine influence unfolding the same divinity in every human heart will become manifest; and then alone shall we be in a position to claim the brotherhood of man.

When a person has reached the highest state of Unity, seeing neither man nor woman, neither sect nor creed, nor color, nor birth, nor any of these differentiations, but goes beyond and finds that One Infinite Spirit behind every human being — only then has that person reached the universal brotherhood, and only then is that person a Vedantist.

There Is Only One Existence

ALL HUMAN KNOWLEDGE proceeds out of experience. Looking around us, what do we experience? A continuous change. The plant comes out of the seed, grows into the tree, completes the circle, and goes back to the seed. The animal comes, lives a certain time, dies, and completes the circle. So does the human being. The mountains slowly but surely crumble away, the rivers slowly but surely dry up, and the rains come out of the sea and then go back to the sea. Everywhere, circles are being completed: birth, growth, development, and decay, each following the other with mathematical precision. This is our everyday experience. Inside of it all, behind all this vast mass of what we call life, of millions of forms and shapes, of millions upon millions of varieties, from the lowest atom to the highest spiritualized individual, we find a certain unity. Every day we find that the wall that was thought to be dividing one thing and another is being broken down, and all matter is coming to be recognized by modern science as one Consciousness manifesting itself in different ways and in various forms; the one Life that runs through all.

What are you and I? You and I are part of the Cosmic Consciousness, or Cosmic Intelligence. This Cosmic Intelligence is what people call Lord or God or Christ or Buddha or Brahman or Spirit; it is what the materialists perceive as force, and what the agnostics call the infinite, inexpressible beyond; and we are all part of that.

The human soul is part of the cosmic energy beyond life and death. Your soul was never born, and it will never die. Birth and death belong to the body only, because the soul is eternal. Standing behind this little universe of nature is the Eternal Soul. There is only One Existence, One Being, the Ever-Blessed, the Omnipresent, the Omniscient, the Birthless, the Deathless. "Through His control the sky expands, through His control the air breathes, through His control the sun shines, and through His control all live." "He is the Reality in nature, He is the Soul of your soul, nay, more, you are He, you are one with Him."

Wherever there are two, there is fear, there is danger, there is conflict, there is strife. When it is all One, who is there to hate, who is there to struggle with? When it is all He, with whom can you fight?

This explains the true nature of life; this explains the true nature of being. As long as you see the many, you are under delusion. "In this world of many, he who sees the One, in this ever-changing world, he who sees Him who never changes as the Soul of his own soul, as his own Self, he is free, he is blessed, he has reached the goal." Therefore, know that you are He; you are one with the God of this universe.

All these small ideas that I am a man or a woman, sick or healthy, strong or weak, or that I hate or love or have little power, are but hallucinations. Stand up then. Know that every thought and word that weakens you in this world is the only evil that exists. Whatever makes us weak and fearful is the only evil that should be shunned. Stand as a rock; you are the Infinite Spirit. Say, "I am Existence Absolute, Bliss Absolute, Knowledge Absolute, I am He," and like a lion breaking its cage, break your chains and be free forever.

What frightens you, what holds you down? Only ignorance of your true nature, of your blessedness; nothing else can bind you. You are the Pure One, the Ever-Blessed. Therefore, if you dare, stand on that — mold your whole life on that. You are one with the Eternal Soul. Know then that thou art He, and model your whole life accordingly; for those who know this and model their lives accordingly will no more suffer in darkness.

The Glory of Our Soul

I HAVE BEEN ASKED TO SAY something about the practical position of the Vedanta philosophy. Theory is very good indeed; but how are we to carry it into practice? If it is absolutely impracticable, no theory is of any value whatever, except as intellectual gymnastics. Vedanta, therefore, as a religion, must be intensely practical. We must be able to carry it out in every part of our lives. The fictitious differentiation between religion and the life of the world must vanish. The ideals of religion must cover the whole field of life; they must enter into all our thoughts, and more and more into practice.

Vedanta teaches Oneness — one life throughout. It preaches the ideal, and the ideal, as we know, is always far ahead of the current state of things, of the practical, as we may call it. Therefore, I ask you to understand that Vedanta, though it is intensely practical, is always so in the sense of the highest ideal. This ideal is that you are, in one word, divine. You are the Infinite Spirit; "Thou art That." This is the essence of Vedanta. The human soul is pure and omniscient; such superstitions as birth and death are nonsense when spoken of in connection with the soul. The soul was never born and will never die.

Vedanta teaches people to have faith in themselves first. As certain religions of the world say that a man who does not believe in a Personal God outside himself is an atheist, so Vedanta says that a man who does not believe in the God within himself is an atheist. Not believing in the glory of our own soul is what Vedanta calls atheism.

To many this is, no doubt, a terrible ideal, and most of us think that this ideal can never be reached; but Vedanta insists that it can be realized by everyone. Nothing can stand as a bar to the realization of this ideal, because, as Vedanta shows, all the powers in the universe are already ours. It is we who put our hands before our eyes and cry that it is dark. Know that there is no darkness around you. Take your hands away and there is the light that was there from the beginning. Darkness never existed; weakness never existed. We who are fools cry that we are weak; we who are fools cry that we are impure. Vedanta insists not only that divinity is our very nature, but that it has been so always. Everything else that you see is false, untrue. As soon as you say, "I am a little mortal being," you are saying something that is not true, you are giving the lie to yourselves, you are hypnotizing yourselves into something weak and wretched. Vedanta recognizes no sin; it recognizes only ignorance. And the greatest ignorance, it says, is to think that you are weak, that you are a sinner, and that you have no power. Every time you think in that way, you rivet one more link in the chain that binds you down, you add one more layer of hypnotism upon your soul. Therefore, whosoever thinks themselves weak is wrong, and whosoever thinks themselves impure is wrong and is throwing bad thoughts into the world.

This we must always bear in mind: In Vedanta, there is no attempt at reconciling the present life — the hypnotized life, this false life that we have assumed — with the ideal; this false life must go, and the Real Life, which has always existed, must manifest itself, must shine out. No one becomes purer and purer; it is only a matter of greater *manifestation* of the perfection that has always been within. The veil drops away, and the native purity of the Eternal Soul begins to manifest itself. Everything is ours already — infinite purity, freedom, love, and power.

Brahman, the God of the Vedanta

BRAHMAN, THE ONE INFINITE Reality of the Vedanta, is the highest generalization to which we can come about God. It has no attributes, but is Existence, Knowledge, and Bliss Absolute. Existence is the very ultimate idea that the human mind can come to. True knowledge does not mean the knowledge of things, but of that One Principle which is expressing itself *through* all things. What is meant by Knowledge is the realization of the essential Unity of things.

The whole universe is simply an ocean of matter, of which you and I are like little whirlpools. Masses of matter are coming into each whirlpool, taking the whirlpool form, and coming out as matter again. The matter that is in my body may have been in yours a few years ago, or in the sun or in a plant, and so on, in a continuous state of flux. So it is with thought. It is an ocean of thought, one infinite mass, in which your mind and my mind are like whirlpools. Are you not seeing the effect now, how my thoughts are entering into yours and yours into mine? The whole of our lives is one.

The essence of matter and thought is Spirit; this is the Unity from which all have come. This grand preaching, the Oneness of all things, making us one with everything that exists, is the great lesson to learn. It is the grand teaching of the Advaita Vedanta. The One Infinite Spirit is the essence of this universe, the essence of all souls. Happiness belongs to those who know this Oneness, who know that they are one with this universe.

Brahman, the God of the Vedanta, has nothing outside of Himself, nothing at all. All this indeed is He. He is everywhere and everything. Him we see and feel; in Him we live and move and have our being. You have that concept in the New Testament. It is the idea of God immanent in the universe, as the very essence, the heart, the soul of all things. He manifests Himself, as it were, in this universe. You and I are little bits, little points, little channels, little expressions, all living inside of that infinite ocean of Existence, Knowledge, and Bliss. The difference between one person and another, between angels and people, between people and animals, between animals and plants, and between plants and stones is not in kind, because everyone from the highest angel to the lowest particle of matter is but an expression of that one infinite ocean, and the difference is only in degree. I am a low manifestation, you may be a higher, but in both, the materials are the same. You and I are both outlets of the One Existence, and that is God; as such, your nature is God, and so is mine. You are of the nature of God by your birthright; so am I. You may be an angel of purity, and I may be the darkest of demons. Nevertheless, my birthright is that infinite ocean of Existence, Knowledge, and Bliss. So is yours. You have manifested yourself more today. But wait; I will manifest myself more yet, for I have it all within me. No extraneous explanation is sought; none is asked for. God Himself is the whole universe, and infinitely more. Is God, then, matter? No, certainly not, for matter is only that infinitesimal part of God able to be perceived by the five senses. God as perceived through the intellect is mind; and when the Spirit sees, He is seen as Spirit. He is not matter, but whatever is real in matter is eternally He.

The Freedom of the Spirit

THE CARDINAL FEATURES of the Hindu religion are founded on the meditative philosophy and the ethical teachings contained in the various books of the Vedas. According to these teachings, innumerable have been the manifestations of the Infinite in the domain of the finite, but the Infinite Spirit Itself is self-existent, eternal, and unchangeable. The passage of time makes no mark whatsoever on the dial of eternity. In the highest region of the Infinite, one that cannot be comprehended at all by human understanding, there is no past and there is no future.

The Vedas teach that the human soul is immortal. The body is subject to the law of growth and decay; what grows must, of necessity, decay. But the indwelling Spirit is the Infinite Life; it never had a beginning and it never will have an end. One of the chief distinctions between the Hindu and the Christian religions is that the Christian religion teaches that each human soul had its beginning at its birth into this world, whereas the Hindu religion asserts that the spirit of the human being is an emanation of the Eternal Being, having had no more a beginning than God Himself. Innumerable have been and will be its manifestations in its passage from one personality to another, subject to the great law of spiritual evolution, until it reaches perfection, when, in Unity, there is no more change.

The mind and the body, in fact all the various phenomena of nature, are in a condition of incessant change. But the highest aspiration of our soul is to find something that does not change, to realize a state of permanent perfection. And this is the aspiration of the soul after the Infinite. The finer our moral and intellectual development, the stronger will become this aspiration after the Eternal.

Our mind and bodies are dependent on the external world, and this dependence varies according to the nature of their relation to it; but the indwelling Spirit is free, as God is free, and it is able to direct, to a greater or lesser degree according to the state of their development, the movements of our minds and bodies.

Death is but a change of condition. We remain in the same universe, and are subject to the same laws as before. Those who have passed beyond and have attained to high planes of wisdom and beauty are but the advance guard of a universal legion that is following after them. The spirit of the highest is always related to the spirit of the lowest, for the germ of infinite perfection exists in all. We should, therefore, cultivate the optimistic temperament, and endeavor to see the good that dwells in everything. If we sit down and lament about the imperfection of our bodies and minds, we profit nothing; it is the heroic endeavor to subdue adverse circumstances that carries our Spirit upward. The object of life is to learn the laws of spiritual progress. Christians can learn from Hindus, and Hindus can learn from Christians. Each has made a contribution of value to the wisdom of the world.

Impress upon your children that true religion is positive and not negative, that it does not consist in merely refraining from evil, but in a persistent performance of noble deeds. True religion comes not from the reading of books; it is the awakening of the Spirit within us, consequent upon pure and heroic action. Every child born into the world brings with it a certain accumulated experience from previous incarnations; and the impress of this experience is seen in the structure of its mind and body. But the feeling of independence that possesses us all shows there is something in us besides mind and body. The soul that reigns within us is independent and creates the desire for freedom. If we are not free, how can we hope to make the world better? We hold that human progress is the result of the action of the human Spirit. The best of what the world is, and of what we ourselves are, are the fruits of the freedom of the Spirit.

We believe in one God, the Father of us all, who is omnipresent and omnipotent, and who guides and preserves His children with infinite love. We believe in a Personal God as the Christians do, but we go further: we believe that we are one with God; that we are God in manifestation, that God is in us, and that we are in God.

We believe there is truth in all religions, and the Hindu bows down to them all; for in this world, truth is to be found not in subtraction, but in addition. We would offer God a bouquet of the most beautiful flowers of all the diverse faiths. We love God for love's sake, not for the hope of reward. We do our duty for duty's sake, not for the hope of reward. We worship the beautiful for beauty's sake, not for the hope of reward. Thus in the purity of our hearts shall we see God. Sacrifices, dogma, mumblings, and mutterings are not religion. They are good only if they stimulate us to lift our thoughts to the apprehension of the Divine Perfection, and our hearts to the brave performances of beautiful and heroic deeds.

Religion Is Realizing God in the Soul

THE SOUL IN ITSELF IS PERFECT. The Old Testament of the Hebrews admits that humanity was perfect at the beginning. We made ourselves impure by our own actions. Some speak of these things in allegories, fables, and symbols. But when we begin to analyze these statements, we find that they all teach that the human soul is in its very nature perfect, and that we are to regain that original purity. How? By knowing God. Knowing God is the aim and goal of all human life.

We find that all religions teach the eternity of the soul, as well as that its luster has been dimmed, and that its original purity is to be regained by the knowledge of God. What is the idea of God in these different religions? The earliest ideas of God were vague. The most ancient nations had different deities — sun, earth, fire, water, and so on. Among the ancients we find numbers of these gods ferociously fighting with one another. Eventually, we find one God standing supreme above all others, but still, different tribes asserted that their one God was the greatest. And they tried to prove it by fighting. The one that could do the best fighting proved thereby that its God was the greatest. Those ideas, of course, were very primitive. But gradually, better and better ideas took the place of the old ones. All those religions were the outgrowth of centuries; not one fell from the skies. Each had to be worked out, bit by bit.

Next came the monotheistic ideas: the belief in only one God, who is omnipotent and omniscient, the one God of the universe. This God is extra-cosmic; He lies in the heavens. We find that the tribal gods have disappeared forever, and this one God of the universe has taken their place: He has become the God of gods. Still, He is only an extra-cosmic God; He is unapproachable, and nothing can come near Him. Then, slowly over time, this idea changes also, and eventually, at the next stage, we find a God imma-nent in nature.

In the New Testament it is taught, "Our Father, who art in heaven" — God living in the heavens separated from humanity. We are living on earth and He is living in heaven. Further on, we find the teaching that He is a God immanent in nature: He is not only God in heaven, but on earth, too. He is the God in us.

However, in the Hindu philosophy we do not stop even there. There is the non-dualistic stage, in which a person realizes that the God he has been worshiping is not only the Father in heaven and on earth, but that "I and my Father are one." He real-izes in his soul that he is God Himself, only a lower expression of Him. All that is real in me is He. The gulf between God and humanity is thus bridged. Thus we see how, by knowing God, we find the kingdom of heaven within us.

These different stages of growth are absolutely necessary to the attainment of purity and perfection. The varying systems of religion are founded on the same ideas. Jesus says, "The kingdom of heaven is within you." Again, he says, "Our father who art in Heaven." How do you reconcile the two sayings? By realizing that He was talking to the uneducated masses when he said the latter, the masses who were uneducated in religion. It was necessary to speak to them in their own language. The masses want concrete ideas, something the senses can grasp. A person may be the great-est philosopher in the world, but a child in religion. Only when we have developed a high state of spirituality can we understand that the kingdom of heaven is within us, that *there* is the real king-dom of the Spirit. Thus we see that the apparent contradictions and perplexities in every religion mark but different stages of growth. There are stages of growth in which forms and symbols are necessary, for they are the language that the souls in that stage can understand.

The next idea that I want to bring to you is that true religion does not consist of doctrines or dogmas. It is not what you read or what doctrines you believe in that is important, but what you *realize*. "Blessed are the pure in heart, for they shall see God," yea, in this life. And that is salvation.

There are those who teach that this can be gained by the mumbling of words. But no great Master ever taught that external forms were necessary for salvation. The power of attaining it is within ourselves. We live and move in God. Creeds and sects have their parts to play, but they are for children, they last but temporarily. No book ever created God, but God inspired all the great books. And no book ever created a soul. We must never forget that. *The aim and end of all religions is the realizing of God in the soul.* That is the one universal religion. If there is one universal truth, one universal goal in all religions, I place it here — in realizing God.

Ideals and methods may differ, but that is the central point. There may be a thousand different radii, but they all converge to the one center, and that is the realization of God: something behind this world of sense, this world of eternal eating and drinking and nonsense, this world of false shadows and selfishness. There is something beyond all books, beyond all creeds, and beyond the vanities of this world, and it is the realization of God within yourself. A man may believe in all the churches in the world, he may carry in his head all the sacred books ever written, he may baptize in all the rivers of the earth; still, if he has no experience of God, I would class him with the atheist. Yet another man may have never entered a church or a mosque or a temple, nor performed any ceremony; but if he feels God within himself and is thereby lifted above the selfish vanities of the world, that man is a truly holy man.

All Is God

ALL THE VARIOUS FORMS of cosmic energy, such as matter, thought, force, and intelligence, are simply the manifestation of that Cosmic Intelligence, or, as we shall call it henceforth, the Supreme Lord. Everything that you see, feel, or hear — the whole universe — is His creation, or, to be a little more accurate, is His projection, or, to be still more accurate, is the Lord Himself. It is He who is shining as the sun and the stars. He is mother earth; He Himself is the ocean. He comes as gentle showers, He is the air that we breathe, and it is He who is working as force in the body. He is the speech that is uttered, and He is the man who is talking. He is the audience that is here. He is the platform on which I stand, and He is the light that enables me to see your faces. It is all He. He Himself is both the material and the efficient cause of this universe, and He it is who becomes involved in the minute cell and evolves at the other end and becomes God again. He it is who comes down and becomes the lowest atom, and slowly unfolding His nature, rejoins Himself.

This is the mystery of the universe. "Thou art the man, Thou art the woman, Thou art the strong walking in the pride of youth, Thou art the old tottering on crutches. Thou art in everything, Thou art everything, O Lord." This is the only solution of the cosmos that satisfies the human intellect. In one sentence: We are born of Him, we live in Him, and unto Him we return.

The Two Ideas of God

THERE ARE TWO IDEAS of God in our scriptures — the one, personal; and the other, impersonal. The idea of the Personal God is that He is the omnipresent Creator, Preserver, and Destroyer of everything, the eternal Father and Mother of the universe, but One who is eternally separate from us and from all souls; and liberation consists in coming near to Him and living in Him. Then there is the other idea of the Impersonal, where all those adjectives are taken away as superfluous and illogical, and there remains an impersonal, omnipresent Being, the One Infinite and Eternal Spirit.

And what is our relationship with this Impersonal Being? According to the Advaita Vedanta, we are He. We and He are one. Every one of us is but a manifestation of this Impersonal Being, who is the very basis of all being, and misery consists in thinking of ourselves as different or separate from Him, and liberation consists in knowing our unity with Him. These, in short, are the two ideas of God that we find in our scriptures.

Some remarks ought to be made here. It is only through the idea of the Impersonal God that you can have any system of ethics. In every nation, the truth has been preached from the most ancient times — love your fellow beings as yourselves. But no reason was forthcoming; no one knew why we should love other beings as ourselves. However, the reason is found right there in the idea of the Impersonal God; you will understand everything when you understand the oneness of the universe. We love other beings as ourselves because the whole world is one, and in hurting anyone, I am hurting myself, and, in loving anyone, I am loving myself. Hence we understand why it is that we should not hurt others. The reason for ethics, therefore, is made clear from this ideal of the Impersonal God.

Then there arises the question of the position of the Personal God within the idea of the Impersonal. I understand the wonderful flow of love that comes from the idea of a Personal God; I thoroughly appreciate the power and potency of Bhakti on people. But what a mine of strength is in this Impersonal God, when all illusions of separation have been thrown overboard, and a person stands and exclaims the truth, "I am the Infinite Spirit!"

Nothing can make us afraid when we stand on the glory of our own soul, the infinite, the eternal, the deathless; that soul before whose magnitude the suns and moons and all their systems appear like drops in the ocean; that soul before whose glory space melts away into nothingness and time vanishes into non-existence. This glorious soul we must believe in. Out of that will come great power.

Whatever you think, that you will be. If you think yourselves weak, weak you will be; if you think yourselves strong, strong you will be; if you think yourselves impure, impure you will be; if you think yourselves pure, pure you will be. This teaches us not to think of ourselves as weak, but as strong, omnipotent, omniscient. No matter that I have not expressed it yet; it is in me. All knowledge is in me, all power, all purity, and all freedom. Why can't I express this knowledge, this power, this purity? Only because I do not yet believe in it. Let me believe in it, and it must and it will come out. This is what the idea of the Impersonal teaches.

Make your children strong from their very childhood; teach them not weakness, nor forms, but make them strong by letting them learn of the glory of their soul. Vedanta has ideas of love and worship and other things that we have in other religions, and more besides; but this idea of the glory of the soul is the most life-giving thought, the most wonderful of all. There and there alone is the great thought that will revolutionize the world and reconcile the knowledge of the material world with religion.

God Reveals Himself to the Pure Heart

LET US SEE HOW THE DOCTRINE of love declared in the Vedas is fully developed and taught in the Bhagavad Gita by Krishna, whom the Hindus believe to have been God incarnate on earth. Krishna taught that a person ought to live in this world like a lotus leaf, which grows in water but is never moistened by the water. So we ought to live in the world — our heart to God and our hands to work.

It is good to love God in the hope of reward in this or the next world, but it is better to love God for love's sake. The prayer goes: "Lord, I do not need wealth or fame or learning. If it is Thy will, I shall go from birth to birth; but grant me this — that I may love Thee without thought of reward, that I may love unselfishly for love's sake."

One of Krishna's disciples, Yudhishthira, was driven from his kingdom by his enemies, and had to take shelter, with his queen, in a forest in the Himalayas. And there one day the queen asked him why it was that he, the most virtuous of men, should suffer so much misery. Yudhishthira answered: "Behold, my queen, the Himalayas — how grand and beautiful they are. I love them. They do not give me anything; but it is my nature to love the grand, the beautiful; therefore I love them. Similarly, I love the Lord. He is the source of all beauty, of all sublimity. He is the only object to be loved. My nature is to love Him, and therefore I love. I do not pray for anything; I do not ask for anything. Let Him place me wherever He likes. I must love Him for love's sake. I cannot trade in love."

The Vedas teach that the soul is divine, only held in the bondage of matter, and that perfection will be reached when this bond bursts. And the word they use for this perfection is *Mukti*, freedom — freedom from the bonds of imperfection, freedom from ignorance, misery, and death. This bondage can only fall off through the mercy of God that comes to the pure alone. God reveals Himself to the pure heart; the pure and the stainless see God, yea, even in this life. Then and only then is all the crookedness of the heart made straight. Then all doubt ceases. Then we are no more the victims of the terrible law of causation.

This is the very center, the most vital concept of Hinduism. The Hindu does not want to live upon words and theories. If there are existences beyond the ordinary sensuous existence, he wants to come face-to-face with them. If there is a soul in him which is not matter, if there is an all-merciful universal Soul, he will go to Him direct. He must see Him; for seeing Him alone can destroy all doubts. So the best proof a Hindu sage gives about the Soul, about God, is that he has seen the Soul; that he has seen God. This is the only condition of perfection. The religion of the Hindus does not consist in struggles and attempts to believe a certain doctrine or dogma, but in *realization*. Thus the whole object of their system is, by constant struggle, to become perfect, to become divine, to reach God and see God everywhere; and this reaching God, this seeing God, this becoming "perfect even as the Father in heaven is perfect," constitutes the religion of the Hindus.

And what becomes of those who attain perfection? They live lives of bliss infinite. They enjoy infinite and perfect bliss, having obtained the only thing in which human beings can find true and lasting pleasure, namely, God, and they enjoy the bliss with God.

So far, all the Hindus are agreed. This is the common religion of all the sects of India. But then perfection is absolute, and the absolute cannot be two or three. And so, when a soul becomes perfect and absolute, it must become one with Brahman, the Infinite Spirit, and it will then realize itself as Existence Absolute, Knowledge Absolute, and Bliss Absolute.

I have often heard this called losing one's individuality. I tell you that it is nothing of the kind. If it is happiness to enjoy the consciousness of this small body, it must be greater happiness to enjoy consciousness beyond the body's limitations, the measure of happiness increasing as consciousness expands, the ultimate happiness being reached when it has become one with Universal Consciousness.

Therefore, to gain this infinite universal individuality, the selfish little individuality must go. Then alone can death cease when I am one with life itself, then alone can misery cease when I am one with happiness itself, then alone can all errors cease when I am one with knowledge itself. Science has proved to me that physical individuality is a delusion, that really my body is one little continuously changing body in an unbroken ocean of matter; and Oneness, Advaita, is the necessary conclusion with regard to my other counterpart, the soul.

The science of religion will become perfect when it discovers Him who is the One Life, the constant and changeless basis of an ever-changing universe, the One who is the only Soul of whom all souls are but temporary manifestations. Thus it is, through multiplicity and duality, that the glory of the eternal Unity is reached.

Maya: The Illusion of Name and Form

THERE IS BUT ONE all-comprehending Existence, and that Existence appears as manifold. This Spirit, or Soul, or Substance is all that exists in the universe. It is, in the language of non-dualism, Brahman, the One Infinite Existence, Consciousness, and Bliss, and It appears to be manifold by the interposition of name and form. Look at the waves in the sea. Not one wave is really different from the sea; so what makes the wave apparently different? Name and form — the form of the wave and the name that we give to it, *wave.* That is what makes it different from the sea. When name and form go, it is the same sea. Who can find any real difference between the wave and the sea? So this whole universe is that One Existence; only the illusions of name and form have created all these seeming differences.

When the sun shines upon millions of globules of water, upon each particle is seen a most perfect representation of the sun. So the one Infinite Spirit, the one Existence of the universe, being reflected on all these numerous globules of varying names and forms, appears to be various; but It is in reality only one. There is no "I" or "you"; it is all one. This idea of duality, of two, is false, and the whole universe, as we ordinarily know it, is the result of this false knowledge. When discrimination comes, we find that there are not two, but one. We find that we are one with this universe as it now exists, as a continuous mass of change. And we find that we are one with That which is beyond all changes, beyond all qualities, eternally perfect, eternally blessed.

There is, therefore, but one Spirit, one Self, eternally pure, eternally perfect, unchangeable. It has never changed; all these various changes in the universe are but appearances in that one Self.

Upon It, name and form have painted all these dreams. It is the form that makes the wave seem different from the sea. When the wave subsides, does the form remain? No, it vanishes. The existence of the wave is entirely dependent upon the existence of the sea, but the existence of the sea is not at all dependent upon the existence of the wave.

Name and form are the outcome of what is called Maya. It is this Maya that creates the illusion of individuals, making one appear different from another. Yet Maya cannot be said to exist. Form cannot be said to exist, because all form depends upon the one ocean of Existence underlying. At the same time, form cannot be said not to exist, seeing that it does makes all this temporary difference. According to the non-dualistic Advaita philosophy, then, this Maya, or ignorance, or name and form is showing us how out of this one Infinite Existence the seeming manifoldness of the universe is projected. As substance, this universe is One. So long as we think that there are two ultimate realities, we are mistaken. When we come to know that there is but One, we are illumined.

You and I, the sun, the moon, and the stars are but the different names of different spots in the same ocean of matter, and this matter is continuously changing in its configuration. The particle of matter that was in the sun several months ago may be in the human being now; tomorrow it may be in an animal; the day after tomorrow it may be in a plant. It is ever coming and going. It is all one unbroken, infinite mass of matter, merely differentiated by names and forms. One point is called the sun; another, the moon; another, the stars; another, a human being; another, an animal; another, a plant — and so on. And all these names are fictitious; they have no reality, because the whole is a continuously changing mass of matter. This very same universe, from another standpoint, is an ocean of thought, where each one of us is a point called a particular mind. You are a mind, I am a mind, everyone is a mind. But the very same universe, viewed from the standpoint of true knowledge, when the eyes have been cleared of delusions and the mind has become pure, appears as the one unbroken Absolute Being, ever pure, unchangeable, and eternal.

Truth Alone Gives Strength

ONE IDEA SEEMS TO BE common to all the Indian systems, and I think to all the systems in the world, whether they know it or not, and that is the divinity of the soul. The human soul is essentially pure and perfect. Its real nature is blessedness and power, not weakness and misery. The one great idea that seems to me to be clear even through masses of superstition in every country and in every religion is the luminous idea that every human soul is divine, that divinity is our true nature.

Whatever hides this truth from us is mere superimposition, as Vedanta calls it. Something has been superimposed, but the divine nature within never dies. In the most degraded, as well as in the most saintly, it is ever present. But it has to be called out in order for it to work itself out. We have to ask, and when we do, it will manifest itself.

We are one with Infinite Existence, we are one with Infinite Knowledge, and we are one with Infinite Bliss. The Sat-Chit-Ananda, the Existence-Knowledge-Bliss Absolute, is the nature of the Soul; and all things and beings that we see in the world are Its expressions, dimly or brightly manifested.

Birth and death, life and decay, degeneration and regeneration are all manifestations of that Oneness. So knowledge, however it manifests itself, either as ignorance or as learning, is but a manifestation of the Soul, the difference being only in degree, and not in kind. The difference in knowledge between the most ignorant person and the greatest genius is only one of degree, and not of kind. The Vedantist thinker boldly says that the enjoyments in this life, even degraded joys, are but different degrees of manifestations of that One Divine Bliss, the Essence of the Soul.

We are not bound; we are free. To say or think that we are bound is dangerous — it is a mistake, it is self-hypnotism. As soon as you say, "I am bound," "I am weak," or "I am helpless," you rivet one more chain upon yourself. Do not say it; do not think it. That is the position of strength. It is weakness, says Vedanta, that is the cause of the misery in this world. We become miserable because we are weak. We lie, steal, kill, and commit other crimes because we are weak. We suffer because we are weak. Where there are no thoughts to weaken us, there is no sorrow. We are miserable through the delusion that we are weak. Give up the delusion, and the whole idea of weakness vanishes.

These are the questions that I put to every man, woman, and child who is in physical, mental, or spiritual training: "Are you strong? Are you getting stronger? Do you feel strength?" For I know that it is Truth alone that gives strength. I know that Truth alone gives life, and nothing but approaching Reality will make us strong. Any system, therefore, which weakens the mind, makes one superstitious, makes one mope, makes one desire all sorts of wild impossibilities, I do not care for, because its effect is dangerous. Strength, therefore, is the one thing needful. Strength is the medicine for the world's disease. Strength is the medicine that the poor must have when tyrannized over by the rich, and strength is the medicine that the ignorant must have when oppressed by the learned. And nothing gives such strength or makes us so moral as this idea of Oneness; nothing makes us work so well, at our best and highest.

"I am Existence, Knowledge, and Bliss Absolute; I am the Blissful One, I am the Blissful One." This, says Vedanta, is the prayer that we should have. This is the way to reach the goal: to continuously tell ourselves that we are divine, that we are the Blissful One. As we go on repeating this, strength comes. We who falter at first will get stronger and stronger, and our strength will increase until Truth takes possession of our hearts and courses through our veins and permeates our bodies. Delusion will vanish as the light within becomes more and more effulgent; load after load of ignorance will vanish, and then will come a time when all else has disappeared, and the Spirit alone shines.

God Is Everywhere as the "I Am"

IT IS NATURALLY THE HARDEST thing for us to understand, this impersonal idea of God, for we are always clinging to the personal. The difference between personal and impersonal God is this: The personal God is only a being, whereas the Impersonal is everything in the universe, and infinitely more besides. "As the one fire coming into the world manifests itself in so many forms, and yet is infinitely more besides," so is the Infinite Spirit.

I have not seen anything but God all my life, nor have you. He is everywhere as the "I am." The moment you feel "I am," you are conscious of the One Existence. Where shall we find God if we cannot see Him in our own hearts and in every living being? "Thou art the man, Thou art the woman, Thou art the girl, and Thou art the boy. Thou art the old man tottering with a stick. Thou art the young man walking in the pride of his strength." Thou art all that exists — a wonderful, living God who is the only fact in and beyond the universe.

This seems to many to be a terrible contradiction of the traditional God, who lives behind a veil somewhere and who nobody ever sees. The priests give us an assurance that if we follow and walk in the way they mark out for us, then, when we die, they will give us a passport to enable us to see the face of God! What are all these ideas of heaven but simply inventions of nonsensical priestcraft?

Vedanta says there is nothing that is not God. The living God is within you and me. The moment I realize God sitting in the temple of every human body, the moment I stand in reverence before every human being and see God in him or her, in that moment everything that binds me vanishes and I am free.

This is the most practical of all worship. It has nothing to do with theorizing or speculation. Yet it frightens many. They say it is not right. They go on theorizing about old ideals told to them by their grandparents, about a God somewhere in heaven. Of course, the Vedanta says that each one of us must have his or her own path, but the path is not the goal. The worship of a God in heaven and all these things are not bad, but they are only steps toward the Truth and not the Truth itself. Some good and beautiful ideas are there, but the Vedanta says at every point, "My friend, He whom you are worshiping as unknown, I worship Him as you. He whom you are seeking throughout the universe has been with you all the time. You are living through Him, for He is the Eternal Witness." He is ever present as the eternal "I"— He existing, the whole universe exists. He is the light and life of the universe. If this "I" were not in you, you could not see; He shining through you, you see the world.

The Blessed Unity

VEDANTA TEACHES THAT the Unity of all existence is already within each of us. None was ever born without it. However you may deny it, it continually asserts itself. For what is human love but more or less an affirmation of that Unity within all: "I am one with thee, my wife, my child, my friend!" Whenever you experience oneness with another, you are affirming the Blessed Unity without knowing it. "The wife loves the husband not for the husband's sake, but for the sake of the Spirit that is in the husband." Whether she realizes it or not, the wife experiences the Unity there.

The whole universe is one existence. There cannot be anything else. Out of diversities we are all going toward this universal existence. Families into tribes, tribes into races, races into nations, nations into humanity — how many wills going to the One! All true knowledge is the realization of this Unity.

The same morality is found throughout all religious systems and ideals. One thing only is preached: "Be unselfish, love others." In the eternal temple of God, in the souls of all beings from the lowest to the highest, it is there — that infinite unselfishness, infinite sacrifice, infinite compulsion to go back to Unity.

We have seemingly been divided and limited because of our ignorance; and we have become, as it were, the little Mrs. So-and-So and Mr. So-and-So. But you are not a little woman or little man cut off from all else; you are the One Universal Existence manifested as you. The soul in its own majesty is rising up every moment and declaring its own intrinsic Divinity.

This Vedanta, this truth, is everywhere, only you must become conscious of it. The masses of foolish beliefs and superstitions hinder us in our progress. If we can, let us throw them off and understand that God is Spirit to be worshiped in Spirit and in truth. The conception of God must be truly spiritual. As we become more and more illumined, we will become strong enough to stand out in the shining light, worshiping the Spirit by the Spirit.

For thousands of years, millions and millions of people all over the world have been taught to consider themselves helpless, sinful creatures who must depend upon the mercy of some external being or beings for salvation. Even at their best, these teachings are but kindergartens of religion. The hour comes when great men and women will arise and cast them off, and make vivid and powerful the true religion, the worship of the Spirit by the Spirit.

You and I Are One with Brahman

ACCORDING TO THE ADVAITA Vedanta theory, all we see around us
— the whole universe, in fact — is the manifestation of the One
Absolute. This is called, in Sanskrit, Brahman. Some of the
Absolute has become changed into the whole of nature. But
here comes a difficulty. How is it possible for the Absolute
to change? What made the Absolute to change? By its very definition, Brahman is unchangeable. Change of the unchangeable
would be a contradiction. The same difficulty applies to those who
believe in a Personal God. How could creation arise out of nothing? Something coming out of nothing can never be.

The answer is that the effect must be the cause in another
form. Out of the seed, the big tree grows. Modern science has
proved beyond doubt that the cause is the effect in another form.
The cause changes and becomes the effect. God has become the
universe. But supposing God *has* become this universe; then God
is here and has changed. And if the Infinite has become this finite
universe, so much of the Infinite has gone, and, therefore, God is
Infinite minus the universe.

To avoid a doctrine of pantheism, where God is no more or
no less than all of nature, there is the very bold theory of the
Vedanta. It states that this universe does not exist as we know and
think of it, and that the unchangeable has not changed in reality
at all. It teaches that the whole of this universe is mere appearance
and not reality; and that this idea of parts and little beings and differentiations is only apparent and not the nature of the thing itself.
God has not changed at all; God has not become the universe at
all. We see God as the universe because we have to look through

time, space, and causation. It is time, space, and causation that make all this seeming differentiation.

The theory of the Vedanta, therefore, comes to this; you and I and everything in the universe *are* the Absolute, not parts, but the whole. All seeming divisions, all limitations, are only apparent. You and I are one with Brahman, complete and perfect, boldly preaches the Vedanta. You were never bound. If you think you are bound, bound you remain; if you know that you are free, free you are. Thus the end and aim of this philosophy is to have us realize that we have been perfect and free always, and that we shall remain perfect and free forever.

The Wisdom of the Vedas

THE HINDUS HAVE RECEIVED their religion through revelation: the Vedas. They hold that the Vedas are without beginning and without end. It may sound ludicrous to this audience that books can be without beginning or end, but by the Vedas no books are meant. They mean the accumulated treasure of spiritual laws discovered by different persons in different times. Just as the law of gravitation existed before its discovery, and would exist if all humanity forgot it, so it is with the laws that govern the spiritual world. The moral, ethical, and spiritual relations between soul and soul and between individual spirits and the Father of all spirits were there before their discovery, and would remain even if we forgot them.

The discoverers of these laws are called Rishis, and we honor them as perfected beings. I am glad to tell this audience that some of the very greatest of them were women.

Here it may be contended that these laws, as laws, may be without end, but they must have had a beginning. The Vedas teach us that creation is without beginning or end, and that God is the ever-active providence, by whose power systems after systems are being evolved out of Himself, made to run for a time, and again destroyed. This is what a Brahmin boy repeats every day: "The sun and the moon the Lord created, like the suns and moons of previous cycles."

Here I stand, and if I shut my eyes and try to conceive my existence, "I," "I," "I," what is the idea before me? The idea of a body. Am I, then, nothing but a combination of material substances? No, the Vedas declare, I am Spirit living in a body. I am not the body. The body will die, but I will not die. Here I am in this body; it will fall, but I will go on living.

Some are born happy, enjoy perfect health, have beautiful bodies, mental vigor, and all their wants supplied. Others are born miserable; some without hands or feet; others, living in profound ignorance, only drag on a wretched existence. Why, if they are all created, does a just and merciful God create one happy and another miserable? Why is He so partial? It will not mend matters in the least to simply say that those who are miserable in this life will be happy in a future one. Why should anyone be miserable, even here, under the reign of a just and merciful God?

The idea of a creator God does not explain this anomaly, but simply asserts the cruel fiat of an all-powerful Being. There must have been other causes, then, before a person's birth, to make him or her miserable or happy; and those causes, the Hindu believes, are their past actions.

We cannot deny that bodies acquire certain tendencies from heredity; but those tendencies only mean the physical configuration through which a particular mind alone can act in a particular way. There are other tendencies peculiar to a soul, caused by its past actions. And a soul with a certain tendency will, by the law of affinity, take birth in that body which is the fittest instrument for the display of that tendency. This is in accord with science, for science wants to explain everything by habit, and habit is acquired through repetition. So repetition is necessary to explain the natural habits of a newborn soul. And because they were not obtained in this present life, they must have come down from past lives.

Taking all this for granted, how is it that I do not remember anything of my past life? This can be easily explained. I am now speaking English. It is not my mother tongue. In fact, no words of my mother tongue are now present in my consciousness; but let me try to bring them up, and they rush in. That shows that consciousness is only the surface of the mental ocean, and that within its depths are stored up all of our experiences. Try and struggle, and they will come up and you will be conscious even of your past life.

So, then, the Hindu believes that he or she is Spirit. The Hindu believes that every soul is a circle whose circumference is nowhere, but whose center is located in the body, and that death means the change of this center from body to body. The Spirit is not bound by the conditions of matter. In its very essence it is free, unbounded, holy, pure, and perfect. But somehow or other, it finds itself tied down to matter and thinks of itself as matter.

Why the free, perfect, and pure Being should be thus under the thraldom of matter is the next question. How can the perfect Soul be deluded into the belief that it is imperfect? How can the pure, the absolute, change even a microscopic particle of its nature? The Hindu is sincere. He is brave enough to face the question honestly, and says, "I do not know. I do not know how the perfect Being, the Soul, came to think of itself as imperfect, as joined to and conditioned by matter." But the fact is a fact for all that. It is a fact in everybody's consciousness that one thinks of oneself as the body and the mind. The Hindu does not attempt to explain why. The answer that it is the will of God is no explanation. It is nothing more than what the Hindu says when he says, "I do not know."

Well, then, the human Spirit is eternal and immortal, perfect and infinite, and death means only a change of center from one body to another. The present is determined by our past actions, and the future by our present actions. The soul will go on evolving up or reverting back, from birth to birth and death to death.

But here is another question: Are we all just tiny boats in a tempest, raised one moment on the foamy crest of a billow, and the next dashed down into a yawning chasm as powerless, helpless wrecks in an ever-raging, ever-rushing, uncompromising current of cause and effect? Are we merely little moths placed under the wheel of causation, which rolls on crushing everything in its way and waits not for the widow's tears or the orphan's cry? The heart sinks at the idea. Yet this cause and effect is the law of nature.

Is there no hope then? "Is there no escape?" was the cry that went up from the bottom of the heart of despair. It reached the throne of mercy, and words of hope and consolation came down and inspired an ancient Vedic sage, and he stood up before the world and in trumpet voice proclaimed the glad tidings: "Hear, ye children of Immortal Bliss! I have found the Infinite One, who is beyond all darkness, all delusion. By knowing Him alone will you be freed from death over again."

"Children of Immortal Bliss" — what a sweet name, what a hopeful name! Allow me to call you, sisters and brothers, by that sweet name — "heirs of Immortal Bliss." Yea, the Hindu refuses to call you sinners. We are the children of God, the sharers of Immortal Bliss, holy and perfect beings. Ye divinities on earth — sinners? It is a sin to call a man so! It is a standing libel on human nature! Come up, O lions, and shake off the delusion that you are sheep; you are souls immortal, spirits free, blessed and eternal; you are not matter, you are not bodies; matter is your servant, not you the servant of matter.

Thus the Vedas proclaim not an endless prison of cause and effect, but the glorious truth that at the head of all natural laws, and in and as every particle of matter and force stands the One Infinite Existence. And what is His nature? He is everywhere, the pure and formless One, the Almighty and All-merciful. "Thou art our Father, Thou art our Mother, Thou art our beloved Friend, Thou art the source of all strength." Thus sang the rishis of the Vedas. And how are we to worship Him? Through love. "He is to be worshiped as the one Beloved, dearer than everything in this and the next life." This is the doctrine of love declared in the Vedas.

Vedanta Dualism

WE FIND THAT THERE ARE three principal variations among the Vedantists. On one point they all agree, and that is that they all believe in God. The first school I will tell you about is styled the dualistic school. The dualists believe that God, who is the creator of the universe and its ruler, is eternally separate from nature and eternally separate from the human soul. God is eternal, nature is eternal, and so are all souls. Nature and the souls become manifested and change, but God remains the same. According to the dualists, this God is a personal God; he is personal in that He has qualities, but not that He has a body. He has human attributes: He is merciful, He is just, He is powerful, He is almighty, He can be approached, He can be prayed to, He can be loved, He loves in return, and so on. In other words, He is a human God, only infinitely greater than human beings are; He has none of the evil qualities that humans have. "He is the repository of an infinite number of blessed qualities" — that is their definition.

The vast mass of Indian people are dualists, worshiping a Personal God. Human nature ordinarily cannot conceive of anything higher. We find that 90 percent of the population of the earth who believe in any religion are dualists. All the religions of Europe and Western Asia are dualistic; they have to be. The ordinary person cannot think of anything that is not concrete. We naturally like to cling to that which our intellect can grasp. That is to say, we can only conceive of higher spiritual ideas by bringing them down to our own level. We can only grasp abstract thoughts by making them concrete. This is the religion of the masses all over the world. They believe in a God who is entirely separate from them: a great king; a high, mighty monarch. At the same time, they make Him purer than the monarchs of the earth; they give Him all good qualities and remove the evil qualities from Him.

With all the dualistic theories, the first difficulty is, how is it possible that under the rule of a just and merciful God, the repository of an infinite number of blessed qualities, there can be so many evils in this world? This question arose in all dualistic religions, but the Hindus never invented a Satan as an answer to it. The Hindus, with one accord, laid the blame on man, and it was easy for them to do so. Why? The answer follows.

We see in this life that we shape and form our future; through our thoughts and actions, everyone of us, every day, shapes the morrow. Today we fix the fate of tomorrow; tomorrow we shall fix the fate of the day after, and so on. And so, it is quite logical that this reasoning can be pushed backward, too. If by our own deeds we shape our destiny in the future, why not apply the same rule to the past? If it be true that we are working out our own destiny here within this short space of time, it must also be true that what we are now is the effect of the whole of our past. Therefore, no other person is necessary to shape the destiny of mankind but man himself. The evils that are in the world are caused by none else but ourselves. We have caused this evil; and just as we can see misery resulting from current evil actions, so also can we see that much of the existing misery in the world is the effect of the past wickedness of man. Therefore, according to this theory, we alone are responsible. God is not to blame. He, the eternally merciful Father, is not to blame at all. "We reap what we sow."

Another peculiar doctrine of Vedantic dualists is that every soul must eventually come to salvation. No one will be left out. Through various vicissitudes, through various sufferings and enjoyments, each one of them will come out in the end. Come out of what? The one common idea of all Hindu sects is that all souls will get out of this universe. According to the dualists, there is beyond this universe a place full of happiness and good only; and when that blessed place is reached, there will be no more necessity of being born and reborn, of living and dying; and this idea is so very dear to them. There will be no disease there, and no death. There will be only eternal happiness, for they will be in the presence of God for all time, and they will enjoy Him forever. They believe that all beings, from the lowest worm up to the highest angels, will all, sooner or later, attain to that world where there will be no more misery. The lower animals will come up and become human, humans will become angels, perhaps then become humans again, and so on, until the time when they will rid themselves of all desire for self-satisfaction, all selfishness, all this clinging on to "me and mine," all this thirsting after life. This "me and mine" is the very root of all the evil in the world. If you ask a dualist, "Is your child yours?" he or she will say, "No, it is God's. My property is not mine, it is God's."

The dualist says that "me and mine" is to be applied to God and God alone; He is the only "me," and everything is His. Everything should be held as God's. When we come to the state where we have no "me and mine," where everything is given up to the Lord, where we love all and are ready to sacrifice everything for the welfare of others without any desire for reward, then our heart will be purified, and when the heart has been purified, into that heart will come the love of God. God is the center of attraction for every soul, and the dualist says, "A needle covered up with clay will not be attracted by a magnet, but as soon as the clay is washed off, it will be attracted." God is the magnet and the human soul is the needle, and its evil works are the dirt and dust that cover it. According to the dualist, as soon as the soul is pure, it will by natural attraction come to God and remain with Him forever, but remain eternally separate. All souls, when they become perfect, become happy forever and live eternally with God. This is the dualistic statement. This is the religion of the masses of India.

Vedanta Qualified Non-Dualism

THE REAL VEDANTA PHILOSOPHY begins with those known as the qualified non-dualists. They make the statement that the effect is never different from the cause; the effect is but the cause reproduced in another form. If the universe is the effect and God the cause, it must be God Himself — it cannot be anything but that. They start with the assertion that God is both the efficient and the material cause of the universe; that He Himself is the Creator, and that He Himself is the material out of which the whole of nature is projected. The word *creation* in your language has no equivalent in Sanskrit, because there is no sect in India that believes in creation as it is regarded in the West, as something coming out of nothing. What we mean by creation is *projection;* projection of that which already existed. The whole universe, according to these qualified non-dualists, is God Himself. He is the material of the universe. We read in the Vedas, "As the spider spins the thread out of its own body, even so the whole universe has come out of the Being."

If the effect is the cause reproduced, then the questions are, How is it that we find this unintelligent material universe produced from a God who is not only immaterial, but who is Eternal Intelligence? How, if the cause is pure and perfect, can the effect be so different? What do these qualified non-dualists say? They say that the three existences — God, nature, and the soul — are one. God is the Supreme Soul, and nature and souls are the body of God. Just as I have a body and I have a soul, so the whole universe and all souls are the body of God, and God is the Soul of souls. Thus, God is the material cause of the universe. The body may change — may be young or old, strong or weak — but that does not affect the Supreme Soul at all. It is always the same Eternal Existence, manifesting through every body. Bodies come and go, but the Soul does not change. Even so, the whole universe is the body of God, and in that sense it *is* God. But the changes in the universe do not affect God.

Now, both the dualists and qualified non-dualists admit that the soul is by its nature pure, but through its own deeds it becomes impure. The qualified non-dualists express it more beautifully than the dualists, by saying that the soul's purity and perfection has become contracted, and what we are now trying to do is to remanifest the intelligence, the purity, and the power which is natural to the soul. Every wicked deed contracts the nature of the soul, and every good deed expands it, and these souls are all parts of God. "As from a blazing fire fly millions of sparks of the same nature, even so from this Infinite Being, God, these souls have come."

The God of the qualified non-dualists is also a Personal God, the repository of an infinite number of blessed qualities, only He is also interpenetrating everything in the universe. He is immanent everywhere and in everything. And when the scriptures say that God is everything, to them it means that God is interpenetrating everything; not that God has become the wall, but that God is in the wall. There is not a particle, not an atom in the universe where He is not. Individual souls are limited; they are not omnipresent. But when they get expansion of their powers and become perfect, there is no more birth and death for them; they live with God forever.

Vedanta Non-Dualism

Now we come to Advaitism, what we believe to be the fairest flower of philosophy and religion that any country in any age has produced, where human thought attains its highest expression and even goes beyond the mystery that seems to be impenetrable. This is the non-dualistic Vedantism. It is too abstruse, too elevated to be the religion of the masses. Even in India, its birthplace, where it has been ruling supreme for the past three thousand years, it has not been able to permeate the masses.

What does the Advaitist declare? He says that if there is a God, that God must be both the material and the efficient cause of the universe. Not only is He the creator, but He is also the created. He Himself *is* this universe. How can that be? God, the Ever-Pure, the Infinite Spirit, has become the universe? Yes, but only apparently so. That which we normally see as the universe does not really exist. But then, what are you and I and all these things we see? Nothing but God. All else is illusion. There is but One Existence, the Infinite, the Ever-Blessed One. It is in that Existence that we dream all these various dreams. It is Brahman, beyond all, the Infinite Spirit, beyond the known and beyond the knowable; in and through That we see the material universe. It is the only Reality. It is this table; It is the audience before me; It is the wall; It is everything, minus the name and form. Take away the form of the table, take away the name; what remains is God.

Everyone and everything is Brahman, the pure, the ever-blessed Infinite Spirit. It is the name and the form that make all the seeming distinctions. If you take away these two differences of name and form, the whole universe is one; there are no two, but one everywhere. You and I are one. There is neither nature nor the universe; there is only that one Infinite Existence, out of which, through name and form, the illusion of all these are manufactured.

How to know the Knower? It cannot be known. How can you see your own Self? You can only reflect yourself. So all this universe is the reflection of that One Eternal Being, and as the reflection falls upon good or bad reflectors, so good or bad images are cast up. Thus in the murderer, it is the reflector that is bad and not the Self. In the saint, the reflector is pure. The Self, the Infinite Spirit, is by Its own nature pure. It is the one Existence of the universe that is reflecting Itself, from the lowest worm to the highest and most perfect being. The whole of this universe is one Unity, one Existence. We are looking upon this one Existence in different forms, and creating all these images upon It. To the being who has limited himself to the condition of man, It appears as the world of man. To the being who is on a higher plane of existence, It may seem like heaven. But there is only one Soul in the universe, not two. It neither comes nor goes. It is neither born nor dies nor reincarnates. How can It die? Where can It go? All these heavens, all these earths, and all these places are just vain imaginations of the mind. They do not exist, never existed in the past, and never will exist in the future.

What does the Advaitist preach? He dethrones all the gods that ever existed or ever will exist in the universe, and places on that throne the Self of every human being, the Atman, higher than the sun and the moon, higher than the heavens, greater than this great universe itself. No books, no scriptures, and no science can ever imagine the glory of the Eternal Spirit that appears as you and I and all of humanity, the only God that ever existed, that exists now, or that ever will exist. "I worship my Spirit," says the Advaitist. To whom else should I bow down? I salute the Spirit, the glory of my soul.

Thus each of us, after our vain search after various gods outside ourselves, completes the circle and comes back to the point from which we started — the human soul. We find that the God who we were searching for in hill and dale, in every temple, and in churches and heavens; that God who we were even imagining as sitting in heaven and ruling the world, is our own Self. I am He and He is I, and the little "I" that I believed to be me never existed.

Yet how could that perfect God have been deluded? He never was. How could a perfect God have been dreaming? He never dreamed. Truth never dreams. Illusion arises from illusion alone. There is no illusion as soon as Truth is seen. You have never been in illusion; it is illusion that has been in you, before you. A cloud is here; another comes and pushes it aside and takes its place. Still another comes and pushes that one away. As before the eternal blue sky, clouds of various hue and color come, remain for a short time, and disappear, leaving it the same eternal blue, even so are you, eternally pure, eternally perfect.

Thus, says the Advaitist, "Know the truth and be free in a moment." All the darkness will then vanish. When we see ourselves as one with the Infinite Being, when all separateness has ceased, when all men and women, all gods and angels, all animals and plants, and the whole universe have melted into that Oneness, then all fear disappears. Who is there to fear? This is the one way, says the Vedantist, to Knowledge. Kill out this differentiation, kill out this superstition that there are many. "He who in this world of many sees that One, he who in this mass of insentiency sees that one Sentient Being, he who in this world of shadows catches that Reality, unto him belongs eternal peace, unto none else."

The Three Stages of Vedanta

I HAVE JUST OUTLINED the salient points of the three steps that Indian religious thought has taken in regard to God. We have seen that it began with the Personal God, the extra-cosmic God. It went from the external God to the internal God immanent in the universe; and it ended in identifying the individual soul itself with that God, making one Soul the Eternal Unity behind all these various manifestations in the universe. This is the last word of the Vedas. It begins with dualism, goes through a qualified monism, and ends in perfect monism. We know how very few in this world can come to the last, or even dare believe in it, and fewer still dare act according to it. Yet we know that therein lies the explanation of all ethics, of all morality, and of all spirituality in the universe. Why is it that everyone says, "Do good to others"? Where is the explanation? Why is it that all great people have preached the brotherhood of man, and greater people the oneness of all lives? Because whether they were conscious of it or not, behind all that, through all of their irrational and personal superstitions, was peering forth the eternal light of the Infinite Spirit, denying all manifoldness and asserting that the whole universe is but one.

Now, as society exists at the present time, all these three stages are necessary; the one does not deny the other, one is simply the fulfillment of the other. The Advaitist or the qualified Advaitist does not say that dualism is wrong; it is a right view, but a lower one. It is on the way to truth. Therefore, let everybody work out their own vision of this universe, according to their own ideas. Injure none, allow people their way; take a person where he or she stands, and, if you can, lend a helping hand and put them on a higher platform, but do not injure and do not destroy. All will come to truth in the long run.

Universal Oneness

IT IS THE DEMOCRATIC GOD that Vedanta teaches. Its God is not the monarch sitting on a throne, entirely apart. There are those who like their God that way; a God to be feared and appeased. They burn candles and crawl in the dust before Him. They want a king in heaven to rule them. Vedanta does not teach this old idea of God at all. In place of that God who sat above the clouds and managed the affairs of the world, who created us out of nothing, and, for some unknown reason, made so many people undergo so much misery, Vedanta teaches the God that is in everyone, that has *become* everyone and everything.

What is the idea of God in a place called heaven? It is materialism. The Vedantic idea of God is the Infinite Principle embodied in every one of us. Does Spirit live only in heaven? What is Spirit? We are all Spirit. Why is it we do not realize it? What makes you different from me? It is our identification with our bodies, and nothing else. Forget the body, see more deeply, and all is Spirit.

What does Vedanta teach us? In the first place, it teaches that you need not even go outside of yourself to know the truth. It teaches that all things are here and now, and that they really are nothing but appearances of the Divine Presence. This Presence is much greater than all the earths and heavens combined. Some people think that this world is bad, and imagine that heaven must be somewhere else. But this world is not bad; this world is God Himself.

Therefore, Vedanta formulates not universal brotherhood, but universal oneness. All is the one Soul throughout. The God of Vedanta is Infinite Being, Impersonal Principle, ever-existent, unchanging, immortal, and we are all His incarnations, His embodiments. This is the God of Vedanta, and His heaven is everywhere. Worship everything as God, for every form is His temple. All else is delusion. You are manifestations of God, all of you. You are incarnations of the Almighty, Omnipresent, Divine Principle. You may laugh at me now, but the time will come when you will understand. You must. Nobody will be left behind.

True Individuality

NOW AND THEN WE KNOW a moment of supreme bliss, when we ask for nothing and we know nothing but joy. Then it passes, and we again see the panorama of the universe moving before us; but we know that it is but a mosaic work set upon God, who is the background of all things.

The Vedanta teaches that Nirvana can be attained here and now, that we do not have to wait for death to reach it. Nirvana is the realization of the Eternal Spirit behind all things; and after having once known that, even if only for an instant, never again can one be deluded by the mirage of multiplicity. Having eyes, we must see the apparent, but all the time we know what it is; we have found out its true nature. It is the screen that hides the Spirit, which is unchanging.

The screen opens, and we find the Eternal behind it. All change is in the screen. In the saint, the screen is thin, and the Reality can almost shine through. In the sinner, the screen is thick, and we are liable to lose sight of the truth that the Spirit is there also, as well as behind the saint's screen. When the screen is wholly removed, we find that it really never existed — that we were the Infinite Spirit and nothing else; even the screen is forgotten.

Those who know the real Self cannot be controlled by anything in nature; they alone can do good to the world. They alone will have seen the real motive of doing good to others, because there is only one. This is the only selflessness; the perception of the universal, and not the illusory individual.

Every case of love and sympathy is, in fact, an assertion of this universal. "Not I, but thou." Help another because you are in him and he is in you; this is the way of seeing it. So the real Vedantist goes on doing good to others, and is never hindered by selfishness. Those who reach this point of selflessness go beyond the moral struggle, beyond everything. They see in the most learned priest, in the cow, in the dog, and in the most miserable places, neither the learned priest, nor the cow, nor the dog, nor the miserable place, but the same divinity manifesting itself in them all. They alone are happy who have acquired that experience of Oneness. Such people are said to be living in God.

It is not that when a person becomes free, he or she will stop and become a dead lump. Such a person will be more active than any other being, because while every other being acts only under compulsion, he or she will act through freedom.

If we are inseparable from God, have we no individuality? Oh yes. Our individuality is God. This is not the individuality you have now; you are coming toward that. Individuality means what cannot be divided. How can you call this ego individuality? One hour you are thinking one way, and the next hour another way, and two hours after, another way. The one true individuality is that which never changes and will never change; and that is the God within us.

The Oneness of Life

"HE, THE ONE, IN HIM all exists. He is near and He is far. He is inside everything, He is outside everything, interpenetrating everything. Whoever sees in every being the One Infinite Spirit, and whoever sees everything in that One Infinite Spirit, he never goes far from that Oneness. Those who see all life and the whole universe in God have no more delusion in them. Where is any more misery for those who see this Oneness everywhere?"

This is the great theme of the Vedanta, this Oneness of life, this Oneness of everything. We shall see how it demonstrates that all our misery comes through ignorance, and this ignorance is the idea of manifoldness, this illusory separation between one human being and another, between one nation and another. Vedanta says this separation does not exist, it is not real. It is merely apparent, on the surface. In the heart of things there is Unity. If you go below the surface, you will find this Unity between all human beings and all races, high and low, rich and poor. If you go deep enough, all will be seen as only variations of the One.

Those who have attained to this conception of Oneness know the reality of everything, the secret of everything. They have traced the reality of everything to the Lord, who is the Center, the Unity of all things, and who is Eternal Existence, Eternal Knowledge, and Eternal Bliss.

They grope in darkness who worship the material world, the world that is produced out of ignorance. And those who live their whole lives in this world without ever finding anything better or higher are groping in still greater darkness. But those who know the secret of nature, those who see everywhere in nature the Oneness that is beyond nature, they alone enjoy Eternal Bliss.

The Universal Religion

AT THE VERY OUTSET, I will tell you that there is no polytheism in India. In every temple, if one stands by and listens, one will find the worshipers applying all the attributes of God, including omnipresence, to the images. It is not polytheism, and it is not idol worshiping. What I have seen, among those that you would call idol worshipers, are people the likes of whom in morality and spirituality and love I have never seen anywhere. A tree is known by its fruits. I stop and ask myself, "Can sin beget holiness?"

Ask why the Hindu uses an external symbol when she worships, and she will tell you that it helps to keep her mind fixed on the One Infinite Being to whom she prays. She knows as well as you do that the image is not God, that it is not omnipresent. After all, how much does omnipresence mean to most of the world? It stands merely as a word, a symbol. Has God superficial area?

By the laws of our mental constitution, we have to associate our ideas of infinity with the image of the blue sky or of the sea; in the same way, we naturally connect our idea of holiness with the image of a church, a temple, a mosque, or a cross. It is true that the Hindus have associated their ideas of holiness, purity, truth, omnipresence, and others with different images and forms. But they do so with this difference: while some people devote their whole lives to their idol of a church or a book and never rise any higher, because to them religion simply means an intellectual assent to certain doctrines, the whole religion of the Hindu is centered in *realization.*

We are to become divine by realizing the divine within us. Idols or symbols or churches or books are only the supports, the helps, of our spiritual childhood; but on and on we must progress.

We must not stop anywhere. "External worship, material worship," say the Hindu scriptures, "is the lowest stage; struggling to rise higher, through mental prayer, is the next stage; but the highest stage is when the Lord has been realized."

If we can realize our divine nature with the help of an image, would it be right to call that a sin? Or, even when we have passed that stage, should we call it an error? To the Hindu, we are not traveling from error to truth, but from truth to truth — from lower to higher truth. All the religions, from the lowest fetishism to the highest absolutism, mean so many attempts of the human soul to grasp and realize the Infinite, each determined by the conditions of its birth and association. Each of these religions marks a stage of progress, and every soul is a young eagle soaring higher and higher, gathering more and more strength, till it reaches the Glorious Sun.

Unity in variety is the plan of nature, and the Hindu has recognized it. Every other religion lays down certain fixed dogmas and tries to force society to adopt them. It places before society only one coat, which must fit Jack and John and Mary all alike. If it does not fit Mary, she must go without a coat to cover her body. The Hindus have discovered that the Absolute can only be thought of, or stated, through the relative, and that the images, crosses, and crescents are simply so many symbols, so many pegs to hang spiritual ideas on. It is not that this help is necessary for everyone; it is certainly not compulsory in Hinduism. But those who do not need it have no right to say that it is wrong.

To the Hindu, the whole world of religion is only a traveling, a coming up of different men and women, through various conditions and circumstances, to the same goal. Every religion is only the evolving of the Infinite Spirit out of the material man; and the same Spirit is the inspirer of all of them. Why, then, are there so many contradictions? They are only apparent, says the Hindu.

The contradictions come from the same truth adapting itself to the varying circumstances of different natures.

It is the same light coming through glasses of different colors. And these little variations are necessary for purposes of adaptation. But in the heart of everything the same Eternal Truth reigns. The Lord has declared to the Hindu, through His incarnation as Krishna, "I am in every religion, like the thread through a string of pearls. Wherever thou seest extraordinary holiness and extraordinary power raising and purifying humanity, know that I am there." And what has been the result? I challenge the world to find, throughout the whole system of Sanskrit philosophy, any such expression that the Hindu alone will be saved and not others.

If there is ever to be a universal religion, it must be one that will have no location in place or time, one that will be infinite, like the God it will preach; one whose sun will shine upon the followers of Krishna and of Christ, on saints and sinners alike; one that will not be Hindu or Buddhist, Christian or Muslim, Jewish or Jain, but the sum total of all these, with infinite space for development; and one that with its catholicity will embrace in its infinite arms every human being, from the lowest to the highest. It will be a religion that will have no place for persecution or intolerance in its polity, that will recognize divinity in every man and woman, and whose whole scope, whose whole force, will be centered in aiding humanity to realize its own true, divine nature.

Offer such a religion and all the nations will follow you. May He who is Brahman of the Hindus, Buddha of the Buddhists, Jehovah of the Jews, Allah of the Muslims, and Father in heaven of the Christians give strength to you to carry out this noble ideal!

Blessed Are the Pure in Heart

THERE ARE THREE WAYS in which human beings perceive God. First, the undeveloped intellect of the uneducated man sees God as being far away, up in the heavens somewhere, sitting on a throne as a great Judge. He looks upon Him with fear. Now you must remember that humanity travels not from error to truth, but from truth to truth — if you like it better, from lower truth to higher truth. All forms of religion, high or low, are just different stages in the upward journey toward the Eternal Light, which is God Himself. Some embody a lower view, some a higher, and that is all the difference. Therefore, the religions of the unthinking masses all over the world have always taught of a God who is outside the universe, who lives in heaven, who governs from that place, who is the punisher of the bad and the rewarder of the good, and so on. As we advance spiritually, we begin to feel that God is omnipresent, that God must be within us, that He must be everywhere, that He is not a distant God, but clearly the Soul of all souls. As my soul moves my body, even so is God the mover of my soul — the Soul within the soul. And then there are a few individuals of pure heart and highly developed mind who go still further, and at last find unity with God. As the New Testament says: "Blessed are the pure in heart, for they shall see God." And they find at last that they and the Father are one.

You will find that these three stages are taught by Jesus. Note the common prayer that he taught: "Our Father, which art in Heaven, hallowed be Thy name," and so on; a simple prayer, mark you, a child's prayer. It is the common prayer because it is intended for the uneducated masses. To a higher circle, to those who had advanced a little more, he gave a more elevated teaching:

"I am in my Father, and ye in me, and I in you." And then, when the Jews asked him who he was, he declared that he and his Father were one. The same thing had been taught by the Jewish Prophets: "Ye are gods; and all of you are children of the Most High." Mark the same three stages.

Jesus came to show the path: that the Spirit is not in forms; that it is not through all sorts of vexations and knotty problems of philosophy that you come to know the Spirit. Better that you had had no learning; better that you had never read a book in your life. These are not at all necessary for salvation — neither wealth nor position nor power nor even learning. But what is necessary is that one thing, *purity.* "Blessed are the pure in heart," for the Spirit in Its own nature is pure. How can It be otherwise? It is of God; It has come from God. In the language of the Bible, "It is the Breath of God."

Can the Spirit of God ever be impure? Of course not! But, alas, it has been covered over with the dust and dirt of ages, through our own actions, good and evil. Various works that were not correct, that were not true, have covered the Spirit with the ignorance of ages. It is only necessary to clear away the dust and dirt, and, when we do, the Spirit will shine immediately. "Blessed are the pure in heart, for they shall see God. . . . The kingdom of heaven is within you." Where goest thou to seek for the kingdom of God, asks Jesus of Nazareth, when it is there within you? Cleanse the Spirit of the impurities that cover it, and you will find it there. It is already yours. It is yours by birthright. You are the heirs of immortality, children of the Eternal Father.

How can you cleanse the Spirit? By renunciation. This is the one ideal Jesus preached, and this has been the ideal preached by all the great Prophets of the world. What is meant by renunciation? Unselfishness. Be selfless. That is the only ideal in morality; perfect unselfishness.

Here is the ideal: when a man has no more of his little self in him, no possessor, nothing to call "me" or "mine," when he has given up that little self to God, destroyed his selfishness — then in that man God is manifest; for in him, all selfish will is gone, crushed out, annihilated. That is the ideal. We cannot reach that state yet; nevertheless, let us worship the ideal and slowly struggle to reach it, though it may be with faltering steps. It may be tomorrow or it may be a thousand years hence, but that ideal has to be reached. For it is not only the end, but also the means. To be unselfish, perfectly selfless, is salvation itself, for the little man within dies, and God alone remains.

One Existence Appearing as Many

THUS FAR WE HAVE SEEN in the theories of the Advaitist philosophers that there is but one Soul; there cannot be two. We have seen how in the whole of this universe there is but One Existence, and that One Existence, when seen through the senses, is called the world of matter. When It is seen through the mind, It is called the world of thoughts and ideas; and when It is seen as It is, then It is the One Infinite Being. It is not that there are three things, matter, mind, and soul; all is the One Soul, seen according to different visions. When knowledge itself comes, all illusions vanish, and we find that it is all nothing but Brahman. I am that One Existence. This is the last conclusion. There are neither three nor two in the universe; it is all One. It is only under the illusion of Maya that the One is seen as many.

When you see yourself as body and mind, then regardless of the truth, you are body and mind and nothing else. This is the current perception of the vast majority of humanity. They may talk of the soul and all these things, but what they perceive is the physical form, the touch, taste, vision, and so on. Only when consciousness rises higher, higher than both body or mind, will we ever see the Reality that is behind shine; only then will we see It as the One Existence-Knowledge-Bliss, the One Soul, the Universal Spirit.

The sum and substance of this lecture is that there is but One Existence, and that One Existence seen through different constitutions appears either as the earth or heaven or hell or gods or ghosts or people or demons or the world. But among the many, "Those who see that One Life in this floating universe, those who realize that One who never changes, unto them belong eternal peace; unto none else, unto none else."

This One Existence has to be realized. The question is, How is it to be realized? How shall we wake up from this dream that we are such small things? We are the Infinite Being of the universe materialized into these little beings, little men and women, so affected by the sweet word of one man, the angry word of another, and so on. What a terrible slavery! If one says a kind word, I begin to rejoice. If another says an angry word, I begin to attack. See my condition — slave of the body, slave of the mind, slave of a good word, slave of a bad word, slave of the senses, slave of everything!

This slavery has to be broken. How? "The Atman has first to be heard of, then reasoned upon, and then meditated upon." This is the method of the Advaita Jnani. The truth has to be heard, then reflected upon, then constantly asserted. Think always, "I am Brahman, I am the Infinite Spirit." Every lesser thought must be cast aside as weakening. Cast aside every thought that says that you are merely a man or a woman. Let body go and let mind go: let everything go but that One Existence.

"I am Brahman." This is to be heard day after day. Everything lesser must be thrown aside; this truth is to be repeated continually, day and night, poured through the ears until it reaches the heart, until every nerve and muscle and drop of blood tingles with the idea that "I am He, I am He." It is the greatest strength; it is religion. These are the words that will burn up the dross that is in the mind, words that will bring out the tremendous energy that is within you already, and words that will awaken the Infinite Power which is sleeping in your heart.

Classical Yoga

—•◆•—

The Pathways to Oneness

SWAMI VIVEKANANDA AT THE PARLIAMENT OF RELIGIONS, CHICAGO, 1893

The Four Yogas

THE ULTIMATE GOAL OF ALL humanity, the aim and end of all religions, is but one — re-union with God, or, what amounts to the same, with the divinity which is every person's true nature. But although the aim is one, the method of attaining it varies with the different temperaments of human beings.

Both the goal and the methods employed for reaching it are called Yoga, a word derived from the same Sanskrit root as the English word *yoke,* meaning "to join," to join us to our reality, God. There are various such Yogas, or methods of union, but the chief ones are Karma Yoga, Bhakti Yoga, Raja Yoga, and Jnana Yoga.

Every person must develop according to his or her own nature. As every science has its methods, so has every religion. The methods of attaining the end of religion are called Yoga by us, and the different forms of Yoga that we teach are adapted to the different natures of people. We classify them in the following way, under four heads:

Karma Yoga — The manner in which we realize our divinity through works and duty.

Bhakti Yoga — The realization of the divinity through devotion to, and love of, a Personal God.

Raja Yoga — The realization of the divinity through the control of mind.

Jnana Yoga — The realization of our divinity through knowledge.

These are all different roads leading to the same center — God. Indeed, the varieties of religious belief are an advantage, because all faiths are good, so far as they encourage us to lead a religious life. The more sects there are, the more opportunities there are for making successful appeals to the divine instinct in all people.

Yoga — Union with God

IN PEOPLE WE SEE SO MANY different natures. There are thousands and thousands of varieties of minds and inclinations. A thorough generalization of them is impossible, but for our practical purpose it is sufficient to have them characterized into four classes. First, there are the active people, the workers; they want to work, and there is tremendous energy in their muscles and their nerves. Their aim is to work — to do charitable deeds, build hospitals, make streets, plan, and organize. Then there are the emotional people, who are able to love deeply the sublime and the beautiful. They love to think of the beautiful, to enjoy the aesthetic side of nature, and to adore Love and the God of Love. They love with their whole heart the great souls of all times, the prophets of religions, and the Incarnations of God on earth; they do not care about the exact date when the Sermon on the Mount was preached or the exact moment of Krishna's birth; what they care for is their personalities, their lovable figures. Such is their ideal. This is the nature of the lover, the emotional person. Then there is the mystic, whose mind wants to analyze its own self, to understand the workings of the human mind, what the forces are that are working inside, and how to know, manipulate, and obtain control over them. This is the mystical mind. Then there is the philosopher, who wants to weigh everything and use his or her intellect to experience even beyond the possibilities of all human philosophy.

Now a religion, in order to satisfy the largest proportion of humanity, must be able to supply food for all these various types of minds; and where this capability is wanting, the existing sects all become one-sided. Suppose you go to a sect that preaches love and emotion. They sing and weep, and preach love. But as soon as you say, "My friend, that is all right, but I want a little reason and philosophy; I want to understand things step-by-step and more rationally," they turn you away. That sect can only help people of an emotional turn of mind. They cannot provide what others need.

Again, there are philosophers who talk of the wisdom of India and the East using big psychological terms. But if a simple person goes to them and says, "Can you tell me anything to make me more spiritual, more loving?" the first thing they would do would be to smile and say, "Oh, first you need to be further along in your reason. What can you understand about spirituality?" Once again, they are only able to help those who are inclined to their way. Then there are the mystical sects who speak all sorts of things about different planes of existence, different states of mind, what the power of the mind can do, and so on. But if you are an ordinary man and say, "Show me the good works that I can do; I am not much given to speculation. Can you give me anything to do that will suit my spiritual needs?" they will smile and say, "Poor man; he doesn't understand the way, he knows so little."

This is the existing condition of religion. What I want to propagate is a religion that will be equally acceptable to all minds; it must be equally philosophical, equally emotional, equally mystical, and equally conducive to action. If professors from the colleges come, scientists and physicists, they will want reason. Let them have it as much as they want. Religion must be able to show them how to realize the philosophy that teaches us that this world is one, that there is but one Existence in the universe. Similarly, if mystics come, we must welcome them, be ready to give them the science of mental analysis, and practically demonstrate it before them. If emotional people come, we must sit, laugh, weep, and "drink the cup of love" with them in the name of the Lord. And if energetic workers come, we must work with them with all the energy that we have. This combination will be the ideal of the nearest approach to a universal religion.

To become harmoniously balanced in all these four directions is my ideal of religion. And this religion is attained by what we, in India, call Yoga — union with God. To the worker, it is union between the individual and the whole of humanity; to the mystic, between the lower and Higher Self; to the lover, union with the God of Love; and to the philosopher, it is the union of all Existence. This is what is meant by Yoga. *Yoga* is a Sanskrit term, and each of these four divisions of Yoga has a different Sanskrit name. The person who seeks after this kind of union is called a Yogi. The workers are called Karma Yogis. Those who seek union through love are called Bhakti Yogis. Those who seek it through mysticism are called Raja Yogis. And those who seek it through philosophy are called Jnana Yogis. So this word *Yogi* comprises them all.

These various Yogas must be carried out in constant practice; mere theories about them will not do any good. First, we have to hear about them, and then we have to think about them. We have to reason the thoughts out, impress them on our minds, and then we have to meditate on them, realize them, until at last they become our whole lives. No longer will religion remain a bundle of ideas or theories, nor merely an intellectual assent; it will enter into our very being. By means of intellectual assent, we may subscribe to many foolish things today, and change our minds altogether tomorrow. But true religion never changes, for true religion is the realization of our divinity, not talk, nor doctrine, nor theories, however beautiful they may be. It is being and becoming, not hearing or acknowledging; it is the whole soul becoming one with the Universal Soul. That is religion.

The Supreme Goal

THE MOMENT YOU ISOLATE yourself, everything hurts. The moment you expand and start to feel for others, you gain. The selfish man is the most miserable man in the world. The happiest man is the man who has destroyed all of his selfishness. In doing so, he has become one with the whole of creation, and God is radiant within him. In all religions, the code of ethics is this: Do not be selfish. Be unselfish. Do things for others! Expand!

The truth is, we are not separate from this universe. Our bodies are simply little whirlpools in the ocean of matter. The sun, the moon, the stars, you and I; all are mere whirlpools. A particular mind is simply a mental whirlpool in the ocean of mind.

In this life, there are two opposite tendencies; one is for the protection of the individuality, and the other is the intense desire to transcend the individuality. The mother sacrifices her own will for the needs of the baby. When she carries the baby in her arms, the call of individuality, or self-preservation, is no more heard. She will go without, but her children will have the best. So for all the people we love, we are ready to sacrifice.

On one hand, we are struggling hard to keep up this individuality; on the other hand, whether we know it or not, we are trying to be free of it. With what result? Tom Brown may struggle hard. He is fighting for all the selfish interests of his individuality. Tom dies and there is not a ripple anywhere upon the surface of the earth. Then there was a Jew born two thousand years ago, and he never moved a finger to keep his individuality. Think of that! He never struggled to protect or feed his individuality. That is why he became the greatest in the world. This is what the world does not realize.

In time, we are to be individuals. But in what sense? What is the true individuality of the human being? Not Tom Brown, but the God within. That is the real individuality. The more we have approached our Spirit, the more we have given up our false individuality. The more we try to collect and gain everything for ourselves, the less we are a true individual. The less we have thought of ourselves, and the more we have sacrificed all individuality during our lifetime, the more we are approaching real individuality. This is the great truth that the world does not understand.

You are men or women now. Do you want to keep your minds as they are now — filled with the angers, ill-wills, jealousies, quarrels, and all the thousand and one small and selfish things that live there? Do you mean to say that you wish to keep them? According to Vedanta philosophy, you cannot; you cannot stop until you are pure and perfect. You cannot stop until you come to the life that never ends; until you become one with life itself.

Many have pleasure as the goal. However, they seek for pleasure only through the senses. But true bliss is found only in the Self, the Spirit. This is the one individuality, the one bliss that never changes, which is eternally perfect. Through sustained discrimination, the great souls of this world found the truth that the false individuality of the senses must go. This ego — the less there is of it, the nearer I am to that which I really am; the Universal Spirit. The less I think of my own individual mind, the nearer I am to the Universal Mind. The less I think of my own soul, the nearer I am to the Universal Soul.

Beliefs, doctrines, or sermons do not make religion. It is the realization, the perception of God alone that is religion. What is the glory of all these saints whom the world reveres? God was no mere doctrine for them. Did they believe because their grandparents believed it? No. It was their realization of the Infinite Spirit, higher and more real than their own bodies, minds, and everything else. We must realize it ourselves. There is no other way.

This realization is the aim of Yoga, and the supreme goal of life. Struggle for it! No temple or church can do it for you. Go to God directly. Then alone will all doubts vanish. Then alone will all crookedness be made straight. In the midst of the manifold, those who see the One Unity; in the midst of death, those who see that One Life; in the midst of the ever-changing, those who see That which never changes in their own soul — unto them belongs eternal peace.

The Great Utility of Divine Realization

SPIRITUAL REALIZATION DOES the greatest good to the world. People are afraid that when they attain it, when they realize that there is but One Infinite Spirit, the fountains of love will be dried up, and all that they love will vanish for them in this life and in the life to come. People never stop to think that the greatest workers in the world have been those who bestowed the least thought on their own little individualities. Then alone do we love when we realize that the object of our love is never any little, mortal thing. Then alone do we love when we see that each of the objects of our love is the veritable God Himself. The wife will love the husband the more when she realizes that the husband is God Himself. The husband will love the wife the more when he knows that the wife is God Himself. The mother will love her children more who sees that the children are God Himself. We will love a holy man more when we know that the holy man is God Himself, and we will also love the unholy man, because we know that the background of even that unholy man is He, the Lord. Those who attain to this knowledge become world-movers, for their little selves are dead, and God stands in their place. The whole universe becomes transfigured to them. That which is painful and miserable will vanish; struggles will depart. Instead of being a prison house, where every day we struggle and fight and compete for a morsel of bread, this universe will then be to us a playground.

This will be the great good to the world resulting from the realization that all is God: If all humanity today were to realize only a bit of that great truth, the whole world would be changed; in place of fighting and quarreling there would be a reign of peace. The indecent and brutal hurry that forces us to fight to get ahead of everyone else would then vanish from the world. With it would vanish all fighting, all hate, and all jealousy. That is the great utility of divine realization. Everything that you see in society will be transfigured then. No more will you stand up and sneeringly cast a glance at a poor man who has made a mistake. No more will you look down with contempt upon the poor woman who walks the street in the night, because you will see even there God Himself. No more will you think of jealousy and punishments. They will all vanish; and love, the greatest ideal of love, will be so powerful that no whip and cord will be necessary to guide humanity aright.

If one-millionth of the men and women who live in this world would simply sit down and for a few minutes say, "You are all God, O ye men and O ye women, you are all the manifestations of the one living Deity!" the whole world would be changed. Instead of projecting currents of jealousy and hatred and evil thought into every corner, in every country people would live in the realization that it is all He.

These ideas were thought and worked out among individuals in ancient times in India. For various reasons, such as the exclusiveness of the teachers and foreign conquest, they were not allowed to spread. Yet they are grand truths, and wherever they have been working, human beings have become divine. My whole life has been changed by the touch of one of these divine souls. The time is coming when these thoughts will be cast abroad over the whole world. Instead of being confined to books of philosophy, instead of being the exclusive possession of sects and of a few of the learned, they will all be broadcast over the whole world, so that they may become the common property of the saint and the sinner, of men and women and children, and of the learned and the ignorant. They will then permeate the atmosphere of the world, and the whole universe, with its countless suns and moons, through everything that speaks, with one voice will say, "All is One, and Thou art That."

Brahman, Karma, and the Soul

GOD IS ETERNALLY CREATING. He is never at rest. His creative energy is working all around us, day and night, and, if it were to stop for a second, the whole universe would fall to the ground. There never was a time when that energy did not work throughout the universe, but there is the law of cycles, *pralaya*. This Sanskrit word, properly translated, is "projection," not "creation." The universe is projected forward by God, and, as such, the whole of nature exists. Then it becomes finer, and, eventually, subsides. After a period of rest, the whole thing is again projected forward, and the same combinations, the same evolutions, the same manifestations appear and remain playing, as it were, for a certain time, only to break again into pieces, to become finer and finer, until the whole thing subsides, rests, and comes out again. Thus it goes on, backward and forward, with a wave-like motion throughout eternity. Time, space, and causation are all within this nature. To say, therefore, that there was a beginning, is nonsense. Wherever in our scriptures the words "beginning" and "end" are used, you must remember that it simply means the beginning and the end of one particular cycle, and no more.

What makes this creation? God. What do I mean by the use of the English word *God?* Certainly not the word as ordinarily used in English — there is a good deal of difference. There is no other suitable word in English, but I would prefer to confine myself to the Sanskrit word *Brahman*. What is Brahman? He is eternal, eternally pure, eternally awake, the almighty, the omnipresent and formless Infinite Spirit. It is He who creates this universe. He is the cause of all these manifestations.

But if He is always creating and holding up this universe, two difficulties arise. We see that there is partiality in the universe. One person is born happy, and another unhappy; one is rich, and another is poor: this shows partiality. Then there is cruelty also, for here the very condition of life is death. One animal tears another to pieces, and every man tries to get the better of his own brother. This competition, this cruelty and horror, is the state of things in this world of ours. If this be the creation of a God, then that God is worse than cruel, worse than any devil that human beings have ever imagined. No, says the Vedanta, it is not the fault of God that this partiality exists, that this competition and cruelty exists. Who makes it? We ourselves. There is a cloud shedding its rain on all fields alike. But it is only the field that is well cultivated that gets the advantage of the shower; another field, which has not been tilled or taken care of, cannot get that advantage. It is not the fault of the cloud. The mercy of God is eternal and unchangeable; it is we who make the differentiation. But how can this difference of some being born happy and some unhappy be explained? They have done nothing to make this difference! No, not in this life, but they did in their last, and the difference is explained by their actions in the previous life.

You see, all Hindus agree that life is eternal. It is not that it has sprung out of nothing, for that cannot be. And so, each one of us is the effect of the past. The child is ushered into the world not as something flashing out of nothing from the hands of nature, as the poets delight so much in depicting, but arrives with a past; and for good or evil, each of us comes to work out our own past deeds. This makes the difference. This is the law of Karma. Each one of us is the maker of our own fate. This law knocks on the head all doctrines of predestination and fate and gives us the only means of reconciliation between God and humanity. We, and none else, are responsible for what we suffer. We are the effects, and we are the causes. We are free therefore. If I am unhappy, it has been of my own making, and that very thing shows that I can be happy if I will. If I am impure, that is also of my own making, and that very thing shows that I can be pure if I will. The human will stands beyond all circumstance. Before the strong, gigantic, and infinite will in every man and woman, all the powers, even of nature, must bow down, succumb, and become its servants. This is the truth of the law of Karma.

The next question, of course, would be, What is the soul? We cannot understand God in our scriptures without knowing the soul. There have been attempts in India, and outside of India, too, to catch a glimpse of the beyond by studying external nature; but instead of giving us a glimpse of the beyond, the more we study the material world, the more we tend to become materialized. The more we handle the material world, the more even the little spirituality that we possessed before starts to vanish. Therefore, this is not the way to spirituality, to knowledge of the Highest; it must come through the heart, the human soul.

The external workings do not teach us anything about the beyond, about the Infinite; it is only the internal that can do so. Only through the soul, therefore, only through the analysis of the human soul, can we come to understand God. There are differences of opinion as to the nature of the human soul among the various sects in India, but there are certain points of agreement. We all agree that souls are without beginning and without end, and immortal by their very nature; also that all powers, purity, omnipresence, and omniscience are buried in each soul. That is a grand idea we ought to remember. In every human being and in every animal, however weak or wicked, great or small, resides the same omnipresent, omniscient Soul. The difference is not in the Soul, but in the manifestation. Between me and the smallest animal, the difference is only in manifestation, but as a principle he is the same as I am, he is my brother, he has the same Soul as I have. This is the greatest principle that India has preached. The talk of the brotherhood of man becomes in India the oneness of universal life — of animals and of all life. Even as our scripture says, "Thus the sage, knowing that the same Lord inhabits all bodies, will worship every body as such."

Those who study the English language are often deluded by the words *soul* and *mind*. Our soul and mind are entirely different things. What we call the mind, the Western people call soul. The body is here, beyond that is the mind, yet behind the mind is the Atman, the soul, the Spirit of humanity. We use the words *Atman* or *Spirit*, or, as Western philosophers have designated it, the word *Self*. Whatever word you use, you must keep it clear that the Atman is separate from the mind, as well as from the body, and that this Atman goes through birth and death accompanied by the mind. And when the time comes that it has manifested itself to perfection, then this going from birth to death ceases for it. Then it is at liberty to remain free throughout all eternity. The goal of the soul is freedom.

The Struggle toward Freedom

THE GRANDEST IDEA in the religion of Vedanta is that we may reach the same goal by different paths of Yoga; and these paths have been generalized into four, namely, those of work (Karma Yoga), love (Bhakti Yoga), psychology (Raja Yoga), and knowledge (Jnana Yoga). But you must remember that these divisions are not well marked, and that each blends into the other. It is not a fact that you can find people who have no other faculty than that of work, or that you can find people who are devoted worshipers only, or that there are those who cultivate nothing but knowledge. These divisions are made in accordance with the type or the tendency that may be seen to prevail in a person. We have found that in the end, all these four paths converge and become one. All religions and all spiritual disciplines lead to the one and the same goal.

I have already tried to point out that goal. It is freedom. Everything that we perceive around us is struggling toward freedom, from the atom to the human being, from the insentient, lifeless particle of matter to the highest existence on earth, the human soul. The world process, in fact, reveals this struggle for freedom. In all combinations, every particle is trying to go its own way, to fly from the other particles; but the others are holding it in check. Our earth is trying to fly away from the sun, and the moon from the earth. Everything has a tendency to infinite dispersion. All that we see in the universe has for its basis this one struggle toward freedom. It is under the impulse of this tendency that the saint prays and the robber robs. When the line of action taken is not a proper one, we call it evil, and when the manifestation of it is proper and high, we call it good. But the impulse is the same: the struggle toward freedom. The saint is oppressed with the knowledge of his condition of bondage, and he wants to get free of it, so he worships God. The thief is oppressed with the idea that he does not possess certain things, and he tries to get rid of the want, to obtain freedom from it; so he steals. Freedom is the one goal of all nature, sentient or insentient. And, consciously or unconsciously, everything is struggling toward that goal. The quality of freedom that the saint seeks is very different from that which the robber seeks; the freedom loved by the saint leads him to the enjoyment of infinite, unspeakable bliss, while that on which the robber has set his heart only forges other bonds for his soul.

Is God's Book Finished?

YOU KNOW THAT THERE are various grades of religious mind. You may be a matter-of-fact, common-sense rationalist: you do not care for forms or ceremonies; you want intellectual, hard, ringing facts, and they alone will satisfy you. Then there are the Muslims, who will not allow a picture or a statue in their place of worship. Very well. But then there are people who are more artistic in temperament. They want a great deal of art — beauty of lines and curves, the colors, flowers, and forms; they want candles, lights, and all the insignia and paraphernalia of ritual so that they may see God. Their minds take God in those forms, as yours takes Him through the intellect. Then, there are the devotional people, whose souls cry for God: they have no other idea but to worship God and to praise Him. Then again, there are the philosophers, standing outside all these, mocking them. They think, "What nonsense! Such ideas about God!"

They may laugh at one another, but each one has a place in this world. All these various minds, all these various types are necessary. If there ever is going to be an ideal religion, it must be broad and large enough to supply food for all these minds. It must supply the strength of philosophy to the philosopher, and the devotee's heart to the worshiper; to the ritualist, it must give all that the most marvelous symbolism can convey, while to the poet, it must give as much of heart as he can take in, and other things besides. To make such a broad religion, we shall have to go back to the time when religions began, and take them all in.

Our watchword, then, will be acceptance, and not exclusion. Not only toleration, for so-called toleration is often blasphemy, and I do not believe in it. I believe in acceptance. Why should I tolerate? Toleration means that I think that you are wrong and I am just allowing you to live. Is it not a blasphemy to think that you and I are *allowing* others to live? I accept all religions that were in the past, and worship with them all; I worship God with every one of them, in whatever form they worship Him. I shall go to the mosque of the Muslim; I shall enter the Christian's church and kneel before the crucifix; I shall enter the Buddhist temple, where I shall take refuge in Buddha and in his Law. I shall go into the forest and sit down in meditation with the Hindu, who is trying to see the Light that enlightens the heart of everyone.

Not only shall I do all these, but I shall keep my heart open for all that may come in the future. Is God's book finished? Or is there still a continuous revelation going on? It is a marvelous book, these spiritual revelations of the world. The Bible, the Vedas, the Koran, and all other sacred books are but so many pages, and an infinite number of pages remain yet to be unfolded. I would leave it open for all of them. We stand in the present, but open ourselves to the infinite future. We take in all that has been in the past, enjoy the light of the present, and open every window of the heart for all that will come in the future. Salutations to all the prophets of the past, to all the great ones of the present, and to all who are to come in the future!

The All-Inclusive Religion

WE HAVE A PECULIAR IDEA in India. Suppose I had a child. I would not teach him any religion, but I would teach him the practice of concentrating his mind, and just one line of prayer — not prayer in your sense, but this: "I meditate on Him who is the Creator of the universe; may He enlighten my mind." Then, when old enough, he goes about hearing the different religious philosophies and teachings, until he finds that which seems the truth to him. He then becomes the disciple of a Guru, or teacher, who is teaching this truth. He may choose to worship Christ or Buddha or Mohammed. We recognize the rights of each of these, and the right of all souls to their own Ishta, or chosen way. It is, therefore, quite possible for my son to be a Buddhist, my wife to be a Christian, and myself a Muslim at one and the same time, with absolute freedom from friction. We are all glad to remember that all roads lead to God; and that the reformation of the world does not depend upon all seeing God through our eyes. Our fundamental idea is that your doctrine need not be mine, nor mine yours. I am my own sect. And you are yours.

We have created a system of religion in India that we believe to be the only truly universal religious system extant; but our belief in its universality rests upon its inclusion of *all* the searchers after God, its absolute charity toward all forms of worship, and its eternal receptivity to those ideas that aid in the full manifestation of God in the universe. We admit the imperfection of our system, because the Reality is beyond all systems; but in this admission lies the portent and promise of an eternal growth. Sects, ceremonies, and books, so far as they are the means to the realization of our divinity, are all right; but when we come to realize the Spirit, all helps are thrown aside. Ritual, hymns, and scriptures, those things through which we have traveled to freedom, vanish for us, and all that remains is "Soham, Soham — I am He, I am He."

We Shall All Reach God

WE MUST ALWAYS APPROACH the study of religion with a reverent attitude. Those who come with a pure heart and a reverent attitude, their heart will be opened, and they will see the truth. If you come with intellect only, you can have some intellectual gymnastics, intellectual theories, but never truth. Truth has such a face that anyone who sees that face becomes convinced. The sun does not require any torch to show it; the sun is self-effulgent. If truth requires evidence, what will evidence that evidence? We can only approach true religion with love and with reverence, and, when we do, our hearts will be able to stand up and say with conviction, "This is truth and this is untruth."

The field of spirituality is beyond our senses. Where is the field of the Spirit? It is beyond the senses, beyond our limited consciousness. Consciousness is only one of the many planes in which we work; you will have to transcend the field of consciousness, transcend the senses, approach nearer and nearer to your own center, and as you do that, you will approach nearer and nearer to God.

What is the proof of God? Direct perception, *pratyaksha*. This perception is no mere sense-perception; it is supersensuous, superconscious, and great training is needed to take us beyond the senses. By means of all sorts of past work and bondages, we are being dragged downward; following the paths of Yoga will make us pure and light. Then bondages will fall off by themselves, and we shall be buoyed up beyond this plane of sense-perception to which we are now tied down, and enter the entirely transcendental realm of true religion.

Every being in the universe has the potentiality of transcending the senses; even the little worm will one day transcend the senses and reach God. No life will be a failure; there is no such thing as failure in the universe. A hundred times we will hurt ourselves, a thousand times we will tumble, but in the end we will all realize our divinity. There will come a time when even the lowest soul will have to go upward. No one will be lost. We are all projected from one common center, which is God. The highest as well as the lowest life that God has ever projected will go back to the Father of all lives. "From whom all beings are projected, in whom all live, and unto whom they all return; that is God."

The Three *Gunas*

ACCORDING TO YOGA PHILOSOPHY, the whole of nature consists of three qualities, or energies, called *Gunas*; one is *Tamas*, another *Rajas*, and the third *Sattva*. These three qualities manifest themselves in the physical world. Tamas is all that is dark, heavy, and inactive. Rajas is activity, attraction, and repulsion. Sattva is calmness and light. Everything that is in nature, all manifestations, are combinations and recombinations of these three forces. In every human being, also, these three materials exist. When the Sattva material prevails, knowledge and illumination comes; when Rajas prevails, activity; and when Tamas prevails, darkness, idleness, and ignorance.

Nature has been divided into these various categories by the Sankhya philosophy; the Spirit is beyond all these, beyond nature. It is effulgent, pure, and perfect. Whatever of intelligence we see in nature is but the reflection of this Spirit upon nature. Nature itself is insentient. You must remember that the word *nature* also includes the mind; mind is in nature, and thought is in nature. From thought down to the grossest form of matter, everything is in nature, everything is a manifestation of nature. This nature has covered the Spirit, and when nature takes away the covering, the Spirit appears in Its own glory.

Yoga: The Pathways Back to God

I SHALL NOW TRY TO DISCUSS one great question, upon which rests the whole theory of religion for the Yogis. It seems the consensus of opinion of the great minds of the world that we are the outcome or manifestation of an absolute condition, back of our present relative condition, and we are going forward, to return to that absolute. This being granted, the question is, Which is better, the absolute or this state? There is no lack of people who think that this manifested state is the highest state. There are thinkers of great caliber who are of the opinion that as manifestations of undifferentiated being, the differentiated state we find ourselves in is a higher state than the absolute. They imagine that in the absolute there cannot be any quality; that it must be insensate, dull, and lifeless; that only this life can be enjoyed, and, therefore, we must cling to it. This means that humanity's goal is the enjoyment of the pleasures of the world; and this world, carried a stage higher by the elimination of its evils, is the ultimate goal that they call heaven. This theory, on the face of it, is absurd. There cannot be good without evil, nor evil without good. To believe in such a world where it is all good and no evil is what Sanskrit logicians call a "dream in the air."

Another theory in modern times has been presented by several schools, which is that humanity's destiny is to go on always improving, always struggling toward but never reaching the goal. This theory of eternal progression is untenable, for destruction is the inevitable end of everything earthly. All of our struggles, hopes, fears, and joys, what will they lead to? They shall all end in death. Nothing is so certain as this. Where, then, is this infinite progression? It is, in reality, only a going out to a distance, and then a coming back to the center from which it started. See how from the gas and dust of space, the sun, moon, and stars are produced; and how they will all eventually dissolve back into it. The same process is happening everywhere. The plant takes material from the earth, eventually dissolves, and gives it back. Every form in this world is taken out of surrounding atoms, and will eventually go back to those atoms. It cannot be that the same law acts differently in different places. Law is uniform. Nothing is more certain than that. Whether we will it or not, we shall, we *have to* return to our origin, which is called God or the Absolute. We all came from God, and we are all bound to go back to God. Call it by any name you like — God, the Absolute, or Nature — the fact remains the same. "From whom all this universe comes out, in whom all that is born lives, and to whom all returns." This is one fact that is certain.

The question again: Is going back to God the higher state or not? The philosophers of the Yoga school emphatically answer that it is. They say that man's present state is a degeneration. There is not one religion on the face of the earth that says we are an improvement. The idea is that our original state is perfect and pure, that we fall until we cannot fall further, and that there must come a time when we shoot upward again. However low we may go, we must ultimately take the upward bend and go back to the original state, the original source, which is God. We come from God in the beginning, in the middle we become human beings, and in the end we go back to God. This is putting it in the dualistic form. The monistic form is that we are God, and go back to Him again.

That which degenerates can never be the highest state. But even so, why should there be so much misery and horror in the world? It is only excusable inasmuch as through it we are able to reach a higher state; that we have to pass through it in order to become whole again. Put a seed into the ground and it disintegrates, dissolves after a time, and out of that dissolution comes the splendid tree. Every soul must disintegrate to become God again. So it follows that the sooner we transcend this current state we call *man* or *woman*, the better for us. Is it by committing suicide that we get out of this state? Not at all. That would make it worse. Torturing ourselves or condemning the world will never get us out. We will have to pass through all of our negativity if we are ever to be free, and the sooner we are through it, the better.

There are much higher states of existence beyond this human state. It is beyond the intellect that the first state of religious life is to be found. When you step beyond thought and intellect and reasoning, then you have made the first step toward God, and that is the beginning of true life. What is commonly called life is but an embryo state.

Your next question might well be, What proof is there that there is a state beyond thought and reasoning that is a higher state? In the first place, the great men and women of the world, those who moved the world, those who never thought of any selfish ends whatever, have declared that this life is but a little stage on the way toward the blissful Infinity that is beyond. In the second place, they not only say so, but they show the way to everyone by explaining their methods so that all can follow in their steps. In the third place, there is no other way left. There is no other reasonable explanation. If we accept, just for a moment, that there is no higher state, what reason could possibly explain the world? The sensible world would be the limit of our knowledge and the goal of our lives if we could not go further. But what reason is there to believe in the testimony of the senses? If reason is all in all, it leaves us no place to stand on this side of nihilism. If we are not committed to believing in anything higher than money, name, or fame, then we are living a fraudulent life.

Kant proclaimed that we cannot penetrate beyond the tremendous dead wall called reason. But that we *can* go beyond reason is the very first idea upon which all Indian thought takes its stand; it dares to seek, and succeeds in finding, something higher than reason, where alone the explanation of our present state is to be found. This is the value of the study of Yoga, the science that will take us beyond the limitations of the senses and reason, to the perfection and purity of our original state. "Thou art our Father, and Thou will take us to the other shore of this ocean of ignorance." This Yoga is the grand science of religion.

Jnana Yoga

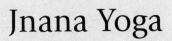

Oneness through Knowledge

SWAMI VIVEKANANDA, CHICAGO, OCTOBER, 1893

The Highest Worship

UNTIL WE SEE NOTHING in the world but the Lord Himself, evils will beset us, and we will continue to make distinctions; for it is only in the Lord, in the Spirit, that we are all one, and until we see God everywhere, this unity will not exist for us. Let us come to that consciousness of the oneness of everything, and let us see ourselves in everything. Let us be no more worshipers with small, limited notions of God, but see Him in and as everything in the universe. Get rid of all these limited ideas and see God in every person — working through all hands, walking through all feet, and eating through every mouth. In every being He lives, through all minds He thinks. To know this is religion. When we feel this oneness, we shall be free.

So long as there is One that breathes throughout the universe, I live in that One. I am not a limited little being; I am one with the universal. I am one with the life of all the children of God. I am one with the soul of Buddha, of Jesus, and of Mohammed.

Stand up then! This is the highest worship. You are one with the universe. That alone is humility — not crawling upon all fours and calling yourself a sinner. The highest creed is Oneness. "I am So-and-So" is a limited idea, not true of the real "I." I am the universal; stand upon that and ever worship the highest, for God is Spirit and should be worshiped in Spirit and in truth.

Through lower forms of worship, humanity's materialistic thoughts rise to spiritual worship, and the Infinite One is at last worshiped. The Spirit alone is infinite. God is Spirit, is infinite; we are Spirit and therefore infinite; and the Infinite alone can worship the Infinite.

The Noble Truth of Unselfishness

IGNORANCE IS THE GREAT MOTHER of all misery, and the fundamental ignorance is to think that the Infinite is finite, that it weeps and cries. This is the basis of all ignorance — that we, the immortal, the ever pure, the perfect Spirit think we are little minds and little bodies. It is the mother of all selfishness. As soon as I think I am a little body, I want to preserve it, to protect it, to keep it nice, at the expense of other bodies. Then you and I become separate. As soon as this idea of separation comes, it opens the door to all mischief and leads to all misery. If but a small fraction of the human beings living today would put aside the idea of selfishness, narrowness, and littleness, this earth would become a paradise overnight. But with improvements of material knowledge only, it will never be so, for these will only increase misery, as oil poured on fire increases the flame all the more. Without the knowledge of the Spirit, all material knowledge is only adding fuel to the fire, only giving into the hands of the selfish man one more instrument to use to take what belongs to others, to live upon the lives of others instead of dedicating his life to them.

Can the knowledge of the Spirit be practiced in modern society? Truth does not pay homage to any society, ancient or modern. Society has to pay homage to truth, or die. Societies should be molded upon truth; truth has not to adjust itself to society. Such a noble truth as unselfishness must be practiced in society if it is to survive.

Stand up, men and women, and in this spirit dare to believe in the truth, dare to practice the truth! Practice that boldness which dares to know the truth, which dares to show the truth in life, which makes us know that we are the Spirit. Then you will be free. Then you will know your real Soul.

Deify the World

TO LIVE IN TRUTH, we must give up error. In order to be good, we must give up evil. Every one of us, in order to have life, must give up what is death. And yet, what remains to us if this involves giving up the material life, the sense life, life as we know it? If we give this up, what remains? I beg to state that in Vedanta alone we find a rational answer to this problem. Here I can only lay before you what Vedanta seeks to teach; and that is the deification of the world.

Vedanta does not denounce the world. The ideal of renunciation nowhere attains such a height as in the teachings of Vedanta. It really means the deification of the world: giving up the world as we think of it, as it appears to us, and seeing it for what it really is. It is God alone; deify it.

We read at the commencement of one of the oldest of the Upanishads: "Whatever exists in this universe is to be covered with the Lord." We have to cover everything with the Lord Himself, not by a false sort of optimism, not by blinding our eyes to evil, but by seeing God in everything. Thus we have to give up our false experience of the world. And when that world is given up, what remains? God.

You can love your wife; it does not mean that you are to abandon her, but you are to see God in your wife. Give up your children — what does that mean? Turn them out of doors? Of course not. But see God in your children. See God in everything. In life and in death, in happiness and in misery, see the Lord equally present. The whole world is full of the Lord. Open your eyes and see Him.

This is what Vedanta teaches: Give up the world that you have conjectured, because your conjecture was based upon a very partial experience. The world we have been clinging to so long is a false world of our own creation. Give that up. Open your eyes and see that, as such, it never existed; it was a dream, Maya. What existed was the Lord Himself. It is He who is in the child, in the wife, and in the husband; it is He who is in the good and in the bad. He is in the sin and in the sinner; He is in life and in death. He is everywhere, expressing Himself as everything. A tremendous assertion indeed! Yet that is the theme that Vedanta wants to demonstrate, to teach, and to preach.

Seeing God in Everything

WE AVOID THE DANGERS of life and its evils by seeing God in everything. What makes us miserable? The cause of the miseries from which we suffer is selfish desire. You desire something for yourself, and when the desire is not fulfilled, the result is distress. If there is no selfish desire, there is no suffering.

The solution is not that you should not have property, not that you should not have things that are necessary or things that are even luxuries. Have all that you want, and more; only know the truth about property and wealth — that it does not belong to anybody. Everything belongs to the Lord. Knowing this, have no idea of proprietorship or possessorship. Instead, see the Lord in everything. God is in the wealth that you enjoy. He is in the desire that rises in your mind. He is in the things that you buy to satisfy your desire; He is in your beautiful attire, and He is in your beautiful ornaments. This is the line of thought. All will be metamorphosed as soon as you begin to see things in that light. If you put God in your every movement, in your conversation, in everything, the whole scene will change, and the world, instead of appearing as a world of woe and misery, will become a heaven.

When we have given up selfish desires, then alone shall we be able to enjoy this universe of God. Then everything will become deified. Nooks and corners, byways and shady places that we thought dark and unholy will all be deified. They will all reveal their true nature. So do your work, says Vedanta; and it advises us how to work: by giving up the apparent, illusive world, by seeing God everywhere.

Thus do your work. Desire to live a hundred years; have all earthly desires, if you wish; only deify them, convert them into heaven. Have the desire to live a long life of helpfulness, of bliss-fulness and activity on this earth. Thus working, you will find the way out. There is no other way. Work, says Vedanta, putting God in everything and knowing Him to be in everything. Work incessantly at holding life as God Himself. God is in everything; where else shall we go to find Him? He is already in every work, in every thought, in every feeling. We have seen how false desires are the cause of all the misery and evil we suffer from; but when they are thus deified, purified through God, they bring no evil, they bring no misery. Those who have not learned this secret do not know what an infinite mine of bliss is in them, around them, and everywhere; they have not yet discovered it.

We are dying of thirst sitting on the bank of the mightiest river. We are dying of hunger sitting near heaps of food. Here is the blissful universe; yet we do not see it. We are in it all the time, and yet we are always misjudging it. The longing for this blissful universe is in all hearts. It is the one goal of religion, and this ideal is expressed in various languages in different religions.

Since my childhood I have been told that I should see God everywhere and in everything, and then I would really enjoy the world; but as soon as I mix with the world and get a few blows from it, the idea vanishes. I am walking in the street thinking that God is in everyone, and a strong man comes along and gives me a push and I fall flat on the footpath. Then I rise up quickly with clenched fist, the blood has rushed to my head, and my discrimination goes. Immediately. I have become mad. Everything is forgotten; instead of encountering God, I see the devil. We have been taught to see God in everything and everywhere; but it is when we come to the practical side that the difficulty begins. But then, if such is the case, what is the use of teaching all these things? There is the greatest use. The use is this; that perseverance will finally conquer. Nothing can be done in a day.

It is thought that is the propelling force in us. Fill the mind with the highest thoughts; hear them day after day, and think them month after month. Never mind failures; they are quite natural. Hold to the ideal a thousand times, and if you fail a thousand times, make the attempt once more. The ideal is to see God in everything. But if you cannot see Him in everything, see Him in one thing, in that thing which you like best, and then see Him in another. And on you will go. There is infinite life before the soul. Take your time and you will achieve your end.

Awake and Arise, Almighty One!

THERE IS ONLY ONE LIFE, and this one Life appears to us to be manifold. This manifoldness is like a dream. The dreams come one after another, and scene after scene unfolds before you, appearing as life. But a time comes to the sage when the whole thing vanishes, and this world, and even his own soul, appears as God Himself. All this manifoldness is the manifestation of that One. That One is manifesting Himself as many — as matter, spirit, mind, thought, and everything else. Therefore, the first step for us to take is to teach this truth to ourselves and to others.

"You are the Pure One. Awake and arise, Almighty One! This sleep does not become you. Almighty One, arise and awake, and manifest your true nature!" Say that to yourself, say it to the world, and see what a practical result follows; see how with an electric flash the truth is manifested, how everything is changed. Tell it to others and show them their power. Then they will learn how to apply it in their daily lives.

To be able to use what we call *viveka*, discrimination, to learn how, in every moment of our lives, in every one of our actions, to discriminate between right and wrong and true and false, we will have to know the test of truth, which is purity, oneness. Everything that makes for oneness is truth. Love is truth, because it makes for oneness; but ill-will is false, because ill-will in any form makes for multiplicity. It is ill-will that separates people; therefore it is wrong and false. It is a disintegrating power; it separates and destroys. Love unites; love makes for that oneness. For love is Existence, God Himself, and all we see is the manifestation of that One Love, more or less expressed. The differences are only of degree; it is the manifestation of that One Love throughout.

Therefore, in all our actions, we have to judge whether or not our act is making for oneness. If it isn't, we have to give it up, but if it is, we may be sure it is good. So with our thoughts; we have to decide whether or not they make for oneness, binding soul to soul and thus generating a great force. If they do this, we will take them up, and if not, we will throw them off as false and harmful to our spiritual growth.

In and through the Infinite Spirit all knowledge comes. Therefore, it is the best known of all. It is your very Self — that which you call "I." You may wonder how this limited "I" can be the unlimited Infinite. But it is so. The limited "I" is a mere fiction. The Infinite has been covered up, as it were, and a little of It is being manifested as the "I" that you presently experience. Limitation, however, can never actually come upon the unlimited; it is a fiction. The Spirit is known, whether we are aware of it or not, to every one of us — every man, woman, and child. Without knowing Him, we could neither live nor move nor have our being; without knowing this Lord of all, we could not breathe or live a second. The God of Vedanta is the most known of all, and is not the outcome of imagination.

Where is there a God more knowable than a God omnipresent in every being, more real than anything we see through our senses? For you and I are He, the Omnipresent God Almighty, and if I say we are not, I tell an untruth. I know it, whether at all times I realize it or not. He is the Eternal Oneness, the Unity of all, the Reality of all life and all existence.

Everyone Is God in Expression

PEOPLE HAVE BEEN WORSHIPING a God in heaven separate from them and of whom they are much afraid. They have been born shaking with fear, and all their lives they will go on shaking. Has the world been made much better by this? How can you expect morality to be developed through fear? It can never be. Love cannot come through fear. When we really begin to love the world, then we understand what is meant by the brotherhood of mankind, and not before.

Vedanta says that the Infinite is our true nature: it will never vanish; it will abide forever. But so long as we have no knowledge of our real nature, we are beggars, jostled about by every force in nature and made slaves by everything in nature. We cry all over the world for help, but help never comes to us. If a king goes mad and runs about trying to find the king of his country, he will never find him, because he is the king himself. He may go through every village and city in his own country, seeking in every house, weeping and wailing, but he will never find him, because he is the king himself.

Through delusion we have been trying to forget our nature, and yet we could not, for it was always calling upon us, and all our search after God or gods, or external freedom was a search after our divinity, our real nature. We mistook the voice. We thought it was from a god beyond, but at last we have found that it was from within ourselves. Within us is this eternal voice speaking of eternal freedom; its music is eternally going on. Part of this music of the Soul has become the earth, the law, and this universe; but it was always ours, and it always will be ours.

The ideal of Vedanta is for human beings to know themselves as they really are; and this is its message: If you cannot worship your brother or sister, the manifested God, how can you worship a God who is unmanifested? Do you not remember what the Bible says: "If you cannot love your brother whom you have seen, how can you love God whom you have not seen?" If you cannot see God in the human face, how can you see Him in the clouds or in images made of dull, dead matter or in the mere fictions of your brain? I shall call you religious from the day you begin to see God in men and women everywhere. When you see men and women as manifestations of God, everything will be welcome. Whatever comes to us is but the Lord, the Eternal, the Blessed One, appearing to us in various forms, as our father, mother, friend, and child — they are all He.

As our human relationships can thus be made divine, so our relationship with God may take any of these forms, and we can look upon Him as our Father or Mother or Friend or Beloved. The culmination of all is to see no difference between lover and beloved. He is in everything; He *is* everything. Every man and woman is the palpable, blissful, living God in expression.

This is to be remembered: those who worship God through ceremonials and forms, however crude we may think them, are not in error. It is the journey from truth to truth, from lower truth to higher truth. Darkness means less light; evil means less good; impurity means less purity. It must always be kept in mind that we should see others with eyes of love, and with sympathy, knowing that they are going along the same path that we have trodden.

Selflessness: The Center of Morality

WHAT ARE THESE IDEAS of religion and God and searching for the hereafter? Why do people in every nation, in every state of society, want a perfect ideal somewhere, either in a man or a woman, or in God, or elsewhere? Because that perfect ideal is within you. It was your own heart beating, and you did not know; you were mistaking it for something external. It is the God within you that is impelling you to seek Him, to realize Him. After long searches here and there, in temples and in churches, in the heavens and on earth, at last you come back to your own soul, completing the circle from where you started, and you find that He whom you have been seeking all over the world, for whom you have been weeping and praying, on whom you were looking as the mystery of all mysteries, shrouded in the clouds, is the nearest of the near, is your own Spirit, the reality of your life, body, and soul.

That Spirit is your own nature. Assert It, manifest It. You are not to become pure; you are pure already. You are not to become perfect; you are that already. Nature is like a screen that is hiding the reality beyond. Every good thought that you think or act upon simply tears the veil, as it were, and the purity, the Infinity, the God behind is manifested more and more. This is the whole history of humanity. Finer and finer becomes the veil, and more and more of the light behind shines forth, for it is its nature to shine.

The Infinite Spirit is the real nature of every human being, and each of us is struggling to express It in various ways. Otherwise, where is the explanation of all ethics? One idea stands out as the center of all ethical systems, expressed in various forms, namely, doing good to others. The guiding motive of humanity should be charity toward men and women, charity toward all beings. But these are simply the various expressions of the eternal truth, "I am one with the universe; this universe is one." It is sympathy, the feeling of sameness everywhere. Even the hardest hearts feel sympathy for other beings sometimes. Even the man who gets frightened if he is told that his small individuality is just a delusion, that it is ignoble to try to cling to it, even that man will tell you that selflessness is at the very center of all morality. And what is this perfect selflessness? It is the abnegation of this apparent self, the renunciation of selfishness.

This idea of "me and mine" is the result of past superstition, and the more the selfish "I" passes away, the more the real "I," the Spirit within, becomes manifest. This is true self-abnegation, the center, the basis of all moral teaching, and whether we know it or not, the whole world is slowly going toward it, practicing it more or less. Only the vast majority of humanity is doing it unconsciously. Let us learn to do it consciously. Let us all make the sacrifice of the selfish "I," knowing that this "me and mine" is not the real Self, but only a limitation. Present man is but a glimpse of the infinite reality that is behind, only a spark of that infinite fire that is the All. The Infinite is our true nature.

What is the utility, the effect, the result of this knowledge? There is the highest utility in this. Happiness, we see, is what everyone is seeking; but the majority of us seek it in things that are evanescent and not real. No happiness was ever found in the senses. Happiness is found only in the Spirit. Therefore, the highest utility for each of us is to find this happiness in the Spirit.

The Real Person Is the Omnipresent Spirit

THE ATMAN, THE INDWELLING SPIRIT, has neither form nor shape; and that which has neither form nor shape must be omnipresent. As Spirit is beyond the mind and formless, it must be beyond time, beyond space, and beyond causation. Now, if it is beyond time, space, and causation, it must be infinite. This leads us to the highest speculation in our philosophy; the Infinite cannot be two. If the Spirit is infinite, there can be only one Spirit, and all ideas of various spirits — of you having one spirit, and I having another, and so forth — cannot be real. The Real Person, therefore, is one and infinite, the one omnipresent Spirit. And the apparent person is only a limitation of that Real Person. In that sense, the mythologies are true in saying that the apparent person, however great he or she may be, is only a dim reflection of the Real Person, who is beyond. The Real Person, the Spirit, being beyond cause and effect, not bound by time or space, must therefore be free. The Real Person was never bound and could not be bound. The apparent person, the reflection, is limited by time, space, and causation, and is therefore bound. Or, in the language of some of our philosophers, the Real Person *appears* to be bound, but really is not. This is the reality in our souls, this omnipresence, this spiritual nature, this infinity.

The body is not the Real Person; neither is the mind, for the mind waxes and wanes. It is the Spirit beyond that alone lives forever. The body and mind are continually changing, and are, in fact, only the names of a series of changeful phenomena, like rivers whose waters are in a constant state of flux, yet who present the appearance of unbroken streams. Every particle in this body is continually changing, and yet we think of it as the same body.

So with the mind: one moment it is happy, another moment unhappy; one moment strong, another weak; an ever-changing whirlpool. That cannot be the Spirit, which is infinite.

People are frightened when they are told that they are the Universal Being, omnipresent and almighty. They worry that they are going to lose their individuality. But what *is* individuality? I should like to see it. If it is in the body, then if I were to lose an eye or one of my hands, some of my individuality would be lost. Then a drunkard should not give up drinking, because he would lose so much of his individuality. This is a very narrow idea of individuality.

There is no individuality except in the Infinite. That is the only condition that does not change. Everything else is in a state of flux. We are not individuals yet. We are struggling toward individuality; and that is the Infinite. That is the real nature of humanity. Those alone live whose lives are in the whole universe; the more we concentrate our lives on limited things, the faster we go toward death. We live in those moments when our lives are in the universe, being lived for others. Living this little life of selfishness is death.

Says an old Sanskrit philosopher, "It is only the Spirit that is the individual, because It is infinite." Infinity cannot be divided; infinity cannot be broken into pieces. It is the same one, undivided Existence forever; and this is the one true Individual, the Real Person. The apparent person is merely a struggle to express and to manifest this individuality, which is the Spirit.

These changes that are going on, such as the wicked becoming good, take them in whatever way you like — they are not occurring in the Spirit. They are the evolution of nature and the greater *manifestation* of the Spirit. Suppose there is a screen hiding you from me, in which there is a small hole through which I can see some of the faces before me, just a few faces. Now suppose that the hole begins to grow larger and larger, and as it does so, more and more of the scene before me reveals itself; when at last the whole screen has disappeared, I stand face-to-face with you all. You did not change at all; it was the hole that was evolving, and you were gradually manifesting yourselves. So it is with the Spirit. No perfection is going to be attained. You, the Infinite Spirit, are already free and perfect.

Have Faith in Your *Self*

THROUGHOUT THE HISTORY of humanity, if any one motive power has been more potent than others in the lives of great men and women, it is that of faith in themselves. Born with the consciousness that they were meant to be great, they became great. We can see that all the difference there is between each of us is due to the existence or non-existence of faith in ourselves. Faith in ourselves will do everything. This is not selfish faith, because Vedanta, again, is the doctrine of oneness. It means faith in all because you are all. You are one with the Eternal Soul, so love for yourself means love for all — love for everything. This is the great faith that will make the world better.

Millions of years have passed since human beings first appeared, and yet but one infinitesimal part of their powers have been manifested. Therefore, you must not believe that you are weak. How do you know what possibilities lie behind the surface? You know but little of that which is within you. For within you is the ocean of infinite power and blessedness.

"The Soul is first to be heard of." Hear day and night that you are that Soul. Repeat it to yourself day and night till it enters into your very veins, till it tingles in every drop of blood, till it is in your flesh and bone. Let the whole body be full of this one idea: "I am the blissful, the omniscient, the ever-glorious Soul." Think of it day and night; think of it till it becomes part and parcel of your life. Meditate upon it. And out of that will come glorious work. Fill yourself with the ideal; remember it well before you take up any work. Then all your actions will be transformed, deified by the very power of this thought. If matter is powerful, thought is omnipotent. Bring this thought to bear upon your life. Fill your-self continuously with the truth of your almightiness, your majesty, and your glory.

Behind All Duality Stands
the Eternal One

"THE SELF-EXISTENT ONE projected the senses outward, and therefore a man looks outward, and not within himself. A certain wise one, desiring immortality, with inverted senses, perceived the Infinite Spirit within." The reality of things is not to be found in the external world; not by looking outward, but by turning the eyes inward. It is He who is within us, the innermost reality of our being, the heart center, the core from which everything comes out; It is He who is the central sun of which the mind, the body, the sense-organs, and everything else we have are but rays going outward.

"People of childish intellect, ignorant persons, run after desires that are external, but the wise never seek for the Eternal in this life of finite things." The Infinite must be sought in that alone which is infinite, and the only thing infinite about us is that which is within us, our own soul. Neither the body, nor the mind, nor even our thoughts, nor the world we see around us are infinite. He to whom they all belong, the Soul of all humanity, He who is awake within each of us, He alone is infinite; and to seek for the Infinite, we must go there. In the Infinite Soul alone we can find it.

In this world we find that all happiness is followed by misery as its shadow. Life has its shadow, death. They must go together, because they are not contradictory, not two separate existences, but different manifestations of the same One, appearing as life and death, sorrow and happiness, good and evil. The dualistic conception that good and evil are two separate entities is false and illusory. They are the diverse manifestations of one and the same

Truth, one time appearing as bad, and at another time as good. The difference does not exist in kind, but only in degree. Beyond and behind all these manifestations, all these seeming contradictions, the Vedanta finds that Unity. Behind all duality stands the Eternal One, the real "you."

You are not the slave of nature. You never were and never will be; this nature, as infinite as you may think it, is only finite, a drop in the ocean, and your Soul is the ocean. You are beyond the stars, the sun, and the moon. They are like mere bubbles compared with your infinite being. Know that, and your whole vision will change. Know that it is you who put your hands before your eyes and say it is dark. Take your hands away and see the light; you are effulgent, you are perfect already, from the very beginning. We now understand the verse, "He goes from death to death who sees the many here. See the One and be free."

How are we to see it? This mind, so deluded, so weak, so easily led, even this mind can be strong enough to catch a glimpse of that knowledge, that Oneness. As rain falling upon a mountain flows in various streams down the sides of the mountain, so all the energies that you see here are from the One Existence. It has become manifold falling upon Maya. Do not run after the manifold; go toward the One. "He is in all that moves; He is in all that is pure; He fills the universe; He is the guest in the house; He is in man, in woman, in water, in animals, in truth; He is the Great One." "As fire coming into this world manifests itself in various forms, even so that One Soul of the universe is manifesting Himself in all these various forms." This will be true for you when you have understood this Unity, and not before. Then you will see Him everywhere.

The question is that if all this is true — that the Pure One, the Soul, the Infinite has entered all this — how is it that He suffers as us, how is it that He becomes miserable, impure? He does not, says the Upanishad. "As the sun is the cause of the eyesight of every being, yet is not made defective by the defect in any eye, even so the Soul of all is not affected by the miseries of the body, or by any misery that is around you."

"He is the One, the Creator of all, the Internal Soul of every being. It is He who makes His Oneness manifold. Those who in this world of evanescence find Him who never changes, those who in this universe of death find that One Life, those who in this manifold find that Oneness, those who realize Him as the Soul of their soul — to those belong eternal peace; unto none else, unto none else."

The highest heaven is in our own soul; the greatest temple of worship is the human soul, greater than all heavens, says the Vedanta; for in no heaven anywhere can we understand the Reality as distinctly and clearly as in our own soul.

I once thought while I was in India that a cave would give me clearer vision. I found it was not so. Then I thought the forest would do so. But the same difficulty existed everywhere, because we make our own world. If I am evil, the whole world is evil to me. That is what the Upanishad says. And so, until I am pure, it is no use going to caves or forests or to heaven. And if I have polished my mirror, it does not matter where I live, because I see the Reality just as It is. It is useless running from place to place, spending energy in vain that should be spent only on polishing the mirror. "None sees Him with the eyes. It is in the mind, in the pure mind, that He is seen, and thus eternal bliss is gained."

The day will come when separation will vanish, and that Oneness to which we are all going will become manifest. A time will come when the harmony of Oneness will pervade the whole world. The whole of mankind will become *Jivanmuktas* — free while living. We are all struggling toward that one end, through our jealousies and hatreds, through our love and cooperation. A tremendous stream is flowing toward the ocean, carrying us all along with it; and though like straws and scraps of paper we may at times float aimlessly about, in the long run we are all sure to join the Ocean of Life and Bliss.

I Am That I Am

EVERYTHING IS SUBSTANCE plus name and form. Name and form come and go, but substance is eternal. All the seeming differentiation in substance is made by the illusion of name and form. Name and form are not real, because they eventually vanish, dissolving back into substance. What we call nature is not substance, because nature is ever-changing and destructible. Nature is time, space, and causation. Nature is Maya.

Maya is the illusion of name and form, into which everything is cast. Maya is not real. We could not destroy it or change it if it were real. Substance is the Spirit, the One Reality behind all temporal phenomena. Maya is simply temporary phenomena. There is the real "me," the Spirit, which nothing can destroy, and there is the phenomenal "me," which is continually changing and disappearing.

Everything existing has these two aspects. One is the unchanging and indestructible Spirit; the other is the ever-changing and destructible phenomena. The true nature of every man and woman is substance, Eternal Spirit. The Spirit never changes, and is never destroyed; but manifested as every thing and every being in the universe, it appears to be clothed with a form and to have a name associated with it. These forms and names continually change and are all eventually destroyed back into substance. Yet people foolishly seek security and peace in their changeable aspects, in the body and the mind.

What is the relationship between nature and me? Insofar as nature stands for name and form or for time, space, and causality, I am not part of nature, because I am free, unchanging, and infinite. However, when the soul molds itself into the cast of name and form, it immediately becomes bound, whereas it was free before. And yet its original nature is always still there. That is why it says, "I am free; in spite of all this bondage, I am free." And it never forgets this.

So when the soul has become bound, nature pulls the strings, and it has to dance as nature wants it to. Thus have you and I danced throughout the years. All the things that we see, do, feel, and know; all of our thoughts and actions, are nothing but dancing to the dictates of nature. There is no freedom in any of this, because none of these pertain to our real Self, the Spirit.

The awakening of the soul to its bondage and its effort to stand up and assert itself — this is the process called life. Success in this struggle is called evolution. The eventual triumph, when all the slavery is blown away, is called salvation, Nirvana, freedom. Everything in the universe is struggling for liberty. When I am bound by nature, by name and form, by time, space, and causality, I do not know what I truly am. But even in this bondage, my Spirit is not completely lost to me. I strain against the bonds; one by one, they break, and I become conscious of my innate grandeur. Then comes liberation. I attain to the clearest and fullest consciousness of myself — I know that I am the Infinite Spirit, master of nature, not its slave. Beyond all differentiation and combination, beyond space, time, and causation, I Am That I Am.

The Tearing of the Screen

WHAT ARE ALL THESE changes in the phenomenal world? This world is an apparent world, bound by time, space, and causation, and it is made of the evolution of nature and the manifestation of the Absolute. The Absolute does not change or re-evolve. Even in the little amoeba, the infinite perfection is latent. It is called amoeba from its amoeba covering, and from the amoeba to the perfect human being, the change is not in what is inside — that eternally remains the same, unchangeable — but the change occurs in the covering.

There is a screen here, and some beautiful scenery outside. There is a small hole in the screen through which we can only catch a glimpse of it. Suppose this hole begins to increase. As it grows larger and larger, more and more of the scenery comes into view, and when the screen has vanished, we come face-to-face with the whole of the scenery. This scene outside is the Infinite Spirit, and the screen between us and the scenery is Maya — time, space, and causation. There is a little hole somewhere, through which I can catch only a glimpse of the soul. When the hole is bigger, I see more and more, and when the screen has vanished, I know that I am the Spirit.

So changes in the universe are not in the Absolute; they are in nature. Nature evolves more and more, until the Absolute manifests Itself. In everyone It exists, although in some It is manifested more than in others. The whole universe is really One. In speaking of the soul, to say that one is superior to another has no meaning. In speaking of the soul, to say that the human being is superior to the animal or the plant has no meaning; the whole universe is the One Soul. In plants, the obstacle to soul manifestation is very great; in animals, a little less; and in people, still less; in cultured, spiritual people, still less; and in perfect people, it has vanished altogether. All our struggles, exercises, pains, pleasures, tears, and smiles, all that we do and think tend toward that goal, the tearing up of the screen, making the hole bigger, thinning the layers that remain between the manifestations and the Reality behind. Our work, therefore, is not to make the soul free, but to get rid of the bondages. The sun is covered by layers of clouds, but remains unaffected by them. The work of the wind is to drive the clouds away, and the more the clouds disappear, the more the light of the sun appears. There is no change whatsoever in the Spirit — for It is the Infinite, Absolute, and Eternal Knowledge, Bliss, and Existence.

Two Birds on the Same Tree

UPON THE SAME TREE there are two birds, one on the top, the other below. The one on the top is calm, silent, and majestic, immersed in his own glory; the one on the lower branches, eating sweet and bitter fruits by turns, hopping from branch to branch, is becoming happy and miserable by turns. After a time, the lower bird eats an exceptionally bitter fruit, and feeling miserable, he looks up and sees the other bird, that wondrous one of golden plumage who eats neither sweet nor bitter fruit, who is neither happy nor miserable, but calm and centered in the Spirit. The lower bird longs for this condition, but soon forgets it, and again begins to eat the fruits. In a little while, he eats another exceptionally bitter fruit, which makes him once again feel miserable, and he again looks up, and he tries to get nearer to the upper bird. Once more he forgets, and after a time he looks up again, and so on he goes again and again, until he comes very near to the beautiful bird and sees the reflection of light from its plumage playing around his own body. He feels a change, and as he comes nearer, he seems to melt away, and everything about him melts away until at last he understands this wonderful change. The lower bird was, as it were, only the shadow, the reflection of the higher; he himself was in essence the upper bird all the time. This eating of fruits, sweet and bitter, this lower, little bird, weeping and happy by turns, was merely a vain dream: all along, the real bird was there above, calm and silent, glorious and majestic, beyond grief, beyond sorrow. The upper bird is God, the Lord of this universe; and the lower bird is the human soul, eating the sweet and bitter fruits of this world.

Now and then comes a heavy blow to the soul. For a time, he stops the eating and goes toward the unknown God, and a flood of light comes. Yet again the senses drag him down, and he begins as before to eat the sweet and bitter fruits of the world. Again, a hard blow comes. Again, his heart becomes open to the divine light; thus gradually he approaches God, and as he gets nearer and nearer, he finds his old self melting away. When he has come near enough, he realizes that he is no other than God, and he exclaims, "He who is the One Life of this universe, as present in the atom as in the suns and the moons — He is the basis of my own life, the Soul of my soul, and I Am That." This is what Jnana Yoga teaches. It teaches us that we are divine. It shows to all humanity the real unity of being, that each one of us is a manifestation on earth of the Lord God Himself. All of us, from the lowest worm to the highest being — all are manifestations of the same God.

You Are Lions

STAND UP, MEN AND WOMEN, and dare to believe in the Truth. "The Atman, the Spirit within, is first to be heard of, then thought about, and then meditated upon." The idea is to fill the brain with only the highest thoughts and the highest ideals; place them day and night before you, and out of that will come great work. We have hypnotized ourselves into thoughts that we are little, and into a constant state of fear.

There is a story about a lioness who was big with child. Going about in search of prey, and seeing a flock of sheep, she jumped upon them. She died in the effort, and a little baby lion was born, motherless. He was taken care of by the sheep, and they brought him up. He grew up with them, ate grass, and bleated like the sheep. And although in time he became a big, full-grown lion, he still thought he was a sheep. One day, another lion came in search of prey and was astonished to find that in the midst of this flock of sheep was a lion, fleeing like the sheep at the approach of danger. He tried to get near the sheep-lion to tell him that he was not a sheep but a lion, but the poor animal fled at his approach. However, he watched his opportunity, and one day found the sheep-lion sleeping. He approached him and said, "You are a lion!" "I am a sheep," cried the other lion; he could not believe the contrary, but bleated. The lion dragged him to a lake and said, "Look here; there is my reflection and there is yours." Then came the comparison. The sheep-lion looked at the lion and then at his own reflection, and in a moment came the idea that he was a lion. The lion roared; the bleating was gone.

You are lions; you are the Spirit, pure, infinite, and perfect. The might of the universe is within you. "Why weepest thou?

Thou art like the infinite sky: clouds of various colors come over it, linger for a moment, then vanish; but the sky is ever the same eternal blue."

Stand Upon the Spirit

AFTER EVERY HAPPINESS comes misery; they may be far apart or near. The more advanced the soul, the more quickly does one follow the other. What we want is neither happiness nor misery. Both make us forget our divinity, our true nature; both are chains — one iron, one gold. Behind both is the Infinite Spirit, who knows neither happiness nor misery. These are just states, and states must ever change; but the nature of the Soul is bliss and peace unchanging. We do not have to get it, we already have it; we only need to wash away the dross to see it.

Stand upon the Spirit; only then can we truly love the world. Take a very, very high stand; we must learn to look with perfect calmness upon all the panorama of the world. It is but baby's play, and when we know this, we will not be disturbed by any of it. If the mind is pleased with praise, it will be displeased with blame. All pleasures of the senses, or even of the mind, are evanescent; but within ourselves is the one source of all true joy, unrelated, dependent upon nothing, perfectly free. *The more we find our bliss there, within us, the more spiritual we are.* The eternal joy of the Spirit is what the world calls religion.

The internal universe, the *real*, is infinitely greater than the external, which is only a shadowy projection of the true one. This world is neither true nor untrue; it is the shadow of truth. We enter into creation and then we give the things of creation life; and then, like fools, we turn around and fear them or run after them endlessly.

The selfish life is just lost equilibrium. What we want is freedom, not just life or pleasure. Life and death are only different names for the same fact, the two sides of the one coin. Both are

Maya. Beyond this is the true nature, the Atman, the Infinite Spirit. It is the Spirit within that we have been worshiping as the God outside of us. It has been our Self all along — the one and only God.

It is the nature of God to be eternally blissful. Let us be one again with God! Make the heart as large as an ocean, going beyond all the trifles of the world. See the world as a picture, and then enjoy its beauty, knowing that nothing affects the real you. Let the whole soul pour in a continuous current to God: seek Him; then will come into your heart that infinite, wonderful bliss of Love. All worldly desires are but beads of glass. Love of God, however, is ever new, and increases every moment we feel it.

We Make Our Own Destiny

I SHALL NOW BRING BEFORE you a point with regard to the theory of reincarnation: It is a theory that advances the freedom of the human soul. It is the one theory that does not lay the blame for all our weakness upon somebody else, which is a common human failing.

We do not look at our own faults. We human beings are very slow to recognize our own weaknesses, our own faults, so long as we can lay the blame upon somebody else. People in general lay blame on other people, or, failing that, on God; or they conjure up a ghost called fate.

Where is fate, and what is fate? We reap what we sow. We are the makers of our own fate. None else has the blame, none else the praise. The wind is blowing; those vessels whose sails are unfurled catch it and go forward on their way, but those that have their sails furled do not catch the wind. Is that the fault of the wind? Is it the fault of the merciful Father, whose wind of mercy is blowing without ceasing, day and night, whose mercy knows no decay — is it His fault that some of us are happy and some unhappy?

We make our own destiny. His sun shines for the weak as well as for the strong. His wind blows for saint and sinner alike. He is the Lord of all, the Father of all, merciful and impartial. Do you mean to say that He, the Lord of creation, looks upon the petty things of our lives in the same light as we do? What a degenerate idea of God that would be! We are like little puppies, making life-and-death struggles here and foolishly thinking that even God Himself will take them as seriously as we do. He knows what puppies' play means. Our attempts to lay the blame on Him, making Him the punisher and the rewarder, are foolish. He neither punishes nor rewards any. His infinite mercy is open to everyone, at all times, in all places, under all conditions, unfailing, unswerving. Upon *us* depends how we utilize it.

Those who blame others — and their number is increasing every day — are generally miserable souls, who have brought themselves to that pass through their own mistakes. Though they blame others, it does not serve them in any way. Blaming others only weakens them the more. Therefore, stand upon your own two feet and take responsibility for your life. Say, "This misery that I am suffering is of my own doing, and that very thing proves that it will have to be undone by me alone. That which I created I can demolish." Therefore stand up, be bold, be strong. Take the whole responsibility on your own shoulders, and know that you are the creator of your own destiny.

All the strength you need is within you. Therefore make your own future. The infinite future is before you, and you must always remember that each word, each thought, and each deed lays up a store for you, and that as the bad thoughts and bad deeds are ready to spring upon you like tigers, so also are the good thoughts and good deeds ready with the power of a hundred thousand angels to defend you always and forever.

The Jnana Yogi

THE JNANA YOGI is the philosopher, the thinker, he who wants to go beyond the visible. He is not satisfied with the little things of this world. His idea is to go beyond the daily routine of eating, drinking, and so on. Not even the teaching of thousands of books will satisfy him. Not even all the sciences or the innumerable systems of worlds will satisfy him; they are to him but a drop in the ocean of existence. His soul wants to go beyond all that into the very heart of being, by seeing Reality as It is; by realizing It, by being It, by becoming one with Universal Being. That is the philosopher. To say that God is the Father or the Mother or the Creator of this universe, or its Protector or Guide is, to him, quite inadequate to express Him. To him, God is the Life of his life, the Soul of his soul. God is his own Spirit. Nothing else remains that is other than God. All the mortal parts of him have been pounded by weighty strokes of knowledge and brushed away. And what at last truly remains is God Himself.

Maya

A LEGEND TELLS HOW ONCE Narada said to Krishna, "Lord, show me Maya." A few days passed, and Krishna asked Narada to make a trip with Him toward a forest. After walking several miles, Krishna said, "Narada, I am thirsty; can you fetch some water for Me?" "I will go at once, Sir, and get you water." So Narada went. At a little distance there was a village. He entered the village in search of water and knocked at a door, which was opened by a most beautiful young girl. At the sight of her, he immediately forgot that his Master was waiting for water, perhaps dying for want of it. He forgot everything and began to talk with the girl. Gradually, that talk ripened into love. He asked the father for his daughter, and they were married and lived there and had children. Thus twelve years passed. His father in-law died; he inherited his property. He lived, as he seemed to think, a very happy life with his wife and children, his fields and his cattle, and so on. Then came a flood. One night the river rose until it overflowed its banks and flooded the whole village. Houses fell, people and animals were swept away and drowned, and everything was floating in the rush of the stream. Narada had to escape. With one hand he held his wife, and with the other, two of his children; another child was on his shoulders, and he was trying to ford this tremendous flood. After a few steps he found that the current was too strong, and the child on his shoulders fell and was swept away. A cry of despair came from Narada. In trying to save that child, he lost his grasp upon the others, and they also were lost. At last his wife, whom he clasped with all his might, was torn away by the current, and he was thrown on the bank, weeping and wailing in bitter lamentation. Behind him there came a gentle voice: "My child, where is the water? You went to fetch a pitcher of water, and I have been waiting for you. You have been gone for quite half an hour." "Half an hour!" Narada exclaimed. Twelve whole years had passed through his mind, and all these scenes had happened in half an hour! This is Maya. And in one form or another, we are all in it.

Stand With the One Who Never Changes

WHEN WE ARE YOUNG and healthy, we think that all the wealth of the world will be ours, and when we get older, after we get kicked about like footballs, we sit in a corner and croak and throw cold water on the enthusiasm of others. Few people know that with pleasure there always comes pain, and with pain, pleasure; that pleasure is the twin brother of pain. It is derogatory to the glory of humanity that a person should go after pain, and equally derogatory that we should only go after pleasure. Both should be turned aside by people whose reason is balanced. Pleasure plays upon us. Pain plays upon us. Why will not men and women seek freedom from being played upon?

One moment we are whipped, and when we begin to weep, nature gives us a dollar, and we are happy for a time; then again we are whipped, and when we weep, nature gives us a piece of gingerbread, and we begin to laugh again. The sage wants liberty from this being played upon; he finds that sense-objects are vain, and that pleasures and pains are never ending. How many rich people in the world are constantly seeking to find fresh pleasures! Pleasures become old, and then they want new ones. Do you not see how many foolish things they are inventing every day, just to titillate the nerves for a moment? When we begin to see the vanity of worldly things, we will feel that we ought not to be thus played upon or led along by nature. That, we see, is slavery.

If a man has a few kind words said to him, he begins to smile, and when he hears a few harsh words, he begins to weep. He is a slave to a bit of bread, a slave to dress, a slave to patriotism, to country, to name, and to fame. He is thus in the midst of slavery, and the spiritual man within him becomes buried, through this bondage. Only when he realizes his slavery does the intense desire to be free come.

God alone is eternal; everything else is transitory. Everything dies; people die, animals die, planets die, suns, moons, and stars all die. Everything in the universe undergoes constant change. The mountains of today were the oceans of yesterday, and will be oceans tomorrow. Everything is in a state of flux. The whole universe is a mass of change. But there is One who never changes, and that is God. And the nearer we get to Him, the less will nature be able to play upon us. And when we finally reach Him and stand with Him, we shall have conquered nature; and these phenomena of nature will no longer have any effect on us.

You see, all knowledge is within us. We really do not require anything else in this world to be free. All perfection is there already in the soul. But this perfection has been covered up by nature; layer after layer of its false knowledge is covering the purity of the soul. What have we to do? I can tell you that we do not have to develop our souls at all. What can develop the already perfect? We must only work to take the veil off; and when we do, the Infinite Spirit within will manifest Itself in Its pristine purity, in Its natural, innate freedom.

Do You Feel for Others?

DO YOU FEEL FOR OTHERS? That is the question. If you do, you are growing in oneness. If you do, the feeling that you have today will become intensified, deified, raised to the highest level, until you experience the oneness in everything, until you feel God in yourself and in others. The intellect can never do that. Intellect is necessary; for without it, we fall into crude errors and make all sorts of mistakes. Intellect checks these. But beyond that, do not try to build anything upon it. It is an inactive, secondary help; the real help is feeling love for others. If you do not feel for others, you may be the greatest intellectual giant ever born, but you will be nothing; you are but dry intellect and you will remain so. And if you do feel for others, even if you cannot read any book and do not know any language, you are on the right path to the Spirit.

It is feeling that is the life, the strength, the vitality; without feeling, no amount of intellectual activity can ever reach God. Feel like Christ and you will become a Christ; feel like Buddha and you will become a Buddha. What is the proof of the Christs and the Buddhas of the world? That you and I feel like them. That is how you and I understand that they were true. Our prophet soul is the proof of their prophet soul. Your godhead is the proof of God Himself. This, says Vedanta, is the ideal to follow. Every one of us will become a prophet. You are one already; only *know it*.

What You Truly Are Is Pure and Perfect

YOU MUST ALWAYS REMEMBER that the central ideal of Vedanta is Oneness. There is but one Life, one Existence. Everything is that One; the differences are of degree and not of kind. The difference between weakness and strength is one of degree. The difference between virtue and vice, heaven and hell, and life and death is one of degree. All differences in this world are of degree, and not of kind, because Oneness is the secret of everything. All is the One, and the One manifests Itself as thought, as life, as soul, as body. This being so, we have no right to look down with contempt upon those who are not developed to the degree we are. If you can stretch out a helping hand, do so; if you cannot, fold your hands, bless your sisters and brothers, and let them go their own way. Dragging down and condemning is not the way to work. Never is work accomplished in that way. We waste our energies in condemning others. Criticism and condemnation are vain and selfish ways of spending our energies.

In our heart of hearts, we all know our weaknesses. But, says Vedanta, being reminded of weakness does not help much. The remedy for weakness is not brooding over weakness, but thinking of strength. Teach people of the strength that is already within them. Instead of telling them that they are sinners, Vedanta takes the opposite position, and says, "What you truly are is pure and perfect, and what you call sin does not belong to you." Sins are simply very low degrees of Self-manifestation; the solution is to manifest your Self in a higher degree. That is the one thing to remember, and all of us can do that. Never say, "I cannot," for you are the Infinite, you are Almighty Spirit.

I Am He

WHY DO WE SEE WICKEDNESS? There was a stump of a tree, and in the dark a thief came that way and said, "That is a policeman." A young man waiting for his beloved saw it and thought it was his sweetheart. A child who had been told ghost stories took it for a ghost and began to shriek. But all the time it was the stump of a tree. We see the world as we are. That which we have inside, we see outside.

Do not talk of the wickedness of the world and all its sins. Weep that you are bound to see wickedness yet, that you are still bound to see sin everywhere. If you want to help the world, do not weaken it more. For what is sin and what is misery but the results of weakness? People are taught from childhood that they are weak and sinners. The world is only made weaker and weaker each day by such teachings. Instead, teach them the truth! Teach them that they are all glorious children of immortality, even those who are the weakest in manifestation. Let positive, strong, helpful thoughts enter into their brains from their very childhood. Lay yourself open to these thoughts, and not to weakening and paralyzing ones. Say to your own mind, "I am the Blissful One. I am the Infinite Spirit. I am He. I am He." Let it ring day and night in your mind like a song, and at the point of death declare, "I am He." That is the Truth. The infinite strength of the world is yours. Drive out the superstition that has covered your mind. Be brave! Know the Truth and practice the Truth, and in time you will realize the Truth perfectly. The goal may be distant, but awake, arise, and stop not till the goal is reached.

He, and He Alone, Should Reign

THE HIGHEST SPIRITUAL WORSHIP is the worship of the Infinite. How grand this idea is, and how difficult to realize! I theorize, talk, and philosophize, and the next moment I come up against something and unconsciously become angry. I forget that there is anything in the universe but this little limited self. I forget to say, "I am the Spirit. What is this trifle to me! I am the Spirit." I forget God; I forget freedom.

One moment I say, "Thy will be done," and the next moment something comes to try me and I lose myself in anger. The goal of all religions is the same, but the language of the teachers differs. The goal is to destroy the selfish "I," so that the real "I," the Lord, will reign through us. "Thou shalt have no other God but Me," say the Hebrew scriptures. We must cherish God alone. We must say, "Not I, but Thou"; not my little personality or any of its selfish clingings, but He, and He alone, should reign.

"Thy will be done" — every moment the traitor mind rebels against it; yet we must say it again and again if we are ever to conquer the lower self. We cannot serve a traitor and be free. There is salvation for all except for the traitor mind, who must be destroyed, and we stand against our own Spirit, against the majesty of God, whenever we refuse to obey the voice of our Higher Self.

You Are the One Existence

IN WORSHIPING GOD we have always been worshiping our own Self. You are one with the Infinite Spirit, and the worst lie that you can tell yourself is that you were born a sinner or wicked. He alone is a sinner who sees a sinner in another person. Suppose there is a baby here, and you place a bag of gold on the table, and then a robber comes and takes the gold away. To the baby it is all the same: because there is no robber inside, the baby sees no robber outside.

The wicked see this universe as hell, and the good see it as heaven, while perfect beings realize it as God Himself. Only when a man sees this universe as God does the veil fall from his eyes; then that man, purified and cleansed, finds his whole vision changed. Thus alone does a man become fearless and free. Then all delusions cease, all fears come to an end. For that man, the whole universe disappears. This surging, moving, continuous struggle of forces stops forever, and that which was manifesting itself as force and matter, as the struggles of nature, as nature itself, as heaven and earth, plants and animals, and men and women — all that becomes transfigured into the one infinite, unbreakable, unchangeable Existence. And then the knowing man finds that he is one with that Existence. "Even as clouds of various colors come before the sky, remain there for a moment, and then vanish away," even so before this soul come all these visions — of earth and heaven, of pleasures and pains; but they all pass away, leaving behind the infinite, unchangeable Spirit. The sky never changes; it is the clouds that change. It is a mistake to think that the Spirit ever changes. It is a mistake to think that we are impure, that we are limited, or that we are separate. The real person within each of us, the authentic Self, *is* the One Existence.

Never Forget What You Really Are

WHAT IS THE PURPOSE of the whole of nature? Why does it exist? It exists so that the Soul may gain experience. The Soul, as it were, has forgotten its mighty, godly nature.

There is a story that the king of the gods, Indra, once became a pig, wallowing in mire; he had a she-pig, and a lot of baby pigs, and he was very happy. Then some gods saw his plight, came to him, and told him, "You are the king of the gods, you have all the gods under your command. Why are you here?" But Indra said, "Never mind; I am all right here; I do not care for heaven while I have this sow and these little pigs." The poor gods were at their wits' end. After a time they decided to slay all the pigs. When all were dead, Indra began to weep and mourn. Then the gods ripped his pig body open, and he came out of it. When he realized what a terrible dream he had had, he started to laugh — he, the king of the gods, to have become a pig, and to have thought that the pig life was the only life! Not only so, but to have wanted the whole universe to come into the pig life!

The Soul, when it identifies itself with nature, forgets that it is pure and infinite. The Soul does not merely love; it is Love itself. It does not exist; it is Existence itself. The Soul does not know; it is Knowledge itself. It is a mistake to say the Soul loves or exists or knows. Love, existence, and knowledge are not the qualities of the Soul, but its *essence*. When they get reflected upon something, you may call them the qualities of that something. However, they are not the qualities, but the essence of the Soul. Somehow the Soul appears to have become so unaware of its perfection that if you approach to tell it, "You are not a pig," it will begin to squeal and bite.

Thus it is with all of us in this Maya, this dream world, where there is so much misery and suffering, where a few golden balls are rolled, and the world scrambles after them. You were never bound by laws. Nature never had a hold on you. That is what the Yogi teaches. Have patience enough to learn it. Understand how the Soul, by identifying itself with the mind and the world, only thinks itself miserable. And know that the only way out of this Maya is through experience. We will have to go through all this experience. We have placed ourselves in this net, and we will have to get ourselves out. We have got ourselves caught in this trap, and we will have to work out our own freedom. So get these experiences of husbands and wives and friends and lesser loves; you will get through them safely if you never forget what you really are. Never forget that this life is only a momentary state, and that we are here to get experience in order to pass through it. Experience is the one great teacher — experience of pleasure *and* pain — but always remember that it is merely experience. It is there only to lead us, step-by-step, to that state where all objects of the senses become small, and the Soul becomes so great and so blissful that the whole universe seems like a drop in the ocean, and falls off by its own nothingness. We have to go through these different experiences, but let us never forget the ideal.

Karma Yoga

Oneness through Selfless Service

SWAMI VIVEKANANDA, SAN FRANCISCO, 1900

Karma Yoga

ALL THE GREAT SYSTEMS of ethics preach absolute selflessness as the goal. Supposing perfect unselfishness can be reached by a person, what becomes of him? He is no more the little Mr. So-and-So; he has acquired infinite expansion. That little personality that he had before is now lost to him forever. He has become infinite; and the attainment of this infinite expansion is indeed the goal of all religions and of all moral and philosophical teachings.

Karma Yoga is the attaining through unselfish work of that blissful freedom which is the goal of all human nature. Every selfish action, therefore, retards our reaching the goal, and every unselfish action takes us toward the goal. That is why the only definition that can be given of morality is this: That which is selfish is immoral, and that which is unselfish is moral.

The goal of all nature is freedom, and freedom is to be attained only by perfect unselfishness; every thought, word, or deed that is unselfish takes us toward the goal, and as such is called moral. That definition, you will find, holds good in every religion and every system of ethics. And yet some persons, in spite of professing this high ethical ideal, are frightened at the thought of having to give up their little personalities. We may ask those who cling to the idea of little personalities to consider the case of a person who has become perfectly unselfish, who has no thought for himself, who speaks no word for himself — and then to ask where his "himself" is. That "himself" is known to him only so long as he thinks, acts, or speaks about himself. If he is only conscious of others, of the universe, and of the all, where is his "himself"? It is gone forever.

Karma Yoga, therefore, is a system of discipline aiming at the attainment of freedom through unselfishness and good works. The Karma Yogi need not believe in any religious doctrine whatsoever. He need not even believe in God or ask what his soul is or think of any metaphysical speculation. He has his own special aim of realizing selflessness, and he has to work it out himself. Every moment of his life must be realization, because he has to solve by mere work and without the help of spiritual doctrine or theory the very same problem to which the Jnani applies reason and the Bhakta applies love.

We can train ourselves, says the Karma Yogi. When the idea of doing good becomes a part of our very being, then we will not seek any motive from outside. Let us do good because it is good to do good; those who do good work even in order to get to heaven bind themselves down, says the Karma Yogi. Any work that is done with selfish motive, instead of making us free, forges one more chain for our feet. On the other hand, every good work we do without any ulterior motive, instead of forging a new link, will break one of the links in the existing chains. Every good thought we send to the world, without thinking of any return, will be stored up and make us purer and purer, until we become the purest of mortals.

Let me tell you in conclusion about a man who actually carried this teaching of Karma Yoga into perfect practice. That man is Buddha. Buddha is the only prophet who said, "I do not care to know your various theories about God. What is the use of discussing all the subtle doctrines about the soul? Do good and be good, and this will take you to freedom and to whatever truth there is." He was, in the conduct of his life, absolutely without personal motive; and what human being worked more than he did? This great philosopher preached the highest philosophy, and yet had the deepest sympathy for all beings and never put forth any claims for himself. He is the ideal Karma Yogi, acting entirely without motive, and the history of humanity shows that he was one of the greatest combinations of heart and brain that ever existed, one of the greatest soul-powers to have ever been manifested. He was the first who dared to say, "Believe not because some old manuscripts are quoted; believe not because you have been made to believe it from your childhood; but reason it all out, and after you have analyzed it and found out that it will do good to one and all, then believe in it, live up to it, and help others to live up to it."

They work best who work without any selfish motive whatsoever. Out of them will come the power to work in such a manner as will transform the world. Such people represent the very highest ideal of Karma Yoga.

Unselfishness Is God

ACCORDING TO KARMA YOGA, the action one has done cannot be destroyed until it has borne fruit; no power in nature can stop it from yielding its results. If I do an evil deed I must suffer for it; there is no power in this universe to stop or stay it. Similarly, if I do a good deed there is no power in the universe that can stop its bearing good results. The cause must have its effect; nothing can prevent or restrain this.

In helping the world, we help ourselves. The main effect of work done for others is that it purifies us. By means of the constant effort to do good to others we are attempting to forget ourselves. This forgetfulness of our little self is the one great lesson we have to learn in life. We foolishly think that through selfish action we can make ourselves happy; but after years of struggle, we find out at last that true happiness consists in destroying selfishness, and that no one can make us happy except ourselves. Every act of charity, every thought of sympathy, every act of help, every good deed takes so much of self-importance away from our little selves.

The highest ideal is self-abnegation, the renunciation of selfishness, where there is no "I," but all is "Thou"; and whether we are conscious of it or not, Karma Yoga leads us to that end. Our ideas of ethics, if they are really good, cannot but be based on selflessness. This is the basis of all morality. It is the one basic idea, the one fundamental principle, running through all ethical systems.

Here are two Sanskrit words. The one is *pravritti*, which means "revolving toward," and the other is *nivritti*, which means "revolving away from." The "revolving toward" is what we call the world of "me and mine." It includes all those things that are always pampering that "me" by wealth and position and power and name and fame, and which are of a grasping nature, always tending to accumulate everything in one small center, that center being "myself." That is pravritti, the natural tendency of every human being — taking everything from everywhere and heaping it around one's own sweet self. When this tendency begins to break and is replaced by nivritti, or "revolving away from," then begins morality and religion. Both pravritti and nivritti are of the nature of work: the former is selfish work, and the latter is selfless work.

Nivritti is the fundamental basis of all morality and religion; and the very culmination of it is selflessness, readiness to sacrifice for another being. When a person has reached that state, he has attained to the ideal of Karma Yoga. This is the highest result of good works. Although he has not studied a single system of philosophy, although he does not believe in any God and never has believed, although he has not prayed even once in his whole life, if the simple power of good actions has brought him to that state where he is selfless toward others, he has arrived at the same point to which the religious person will come through her prayers and the philosopher through his knowledge. So you find that the philosopher, the worker, and the devotee all meet at one point, that one point being self-abnegation, the renunciation of selfishness.

However much the various systems of philosophy and religion may differ, all humanity stands in reverence and awe before those who are ready to sacrifice themselves for others. Here it is not at all a question of creed or doctrine. Even people who are very much opposed to all religious ideas, when they see one of these acts of self-sacrifice, feel that they must revere it.

The worshiper, by keeping constantly before him or her the idea of God, comes to the same point at last and says, "Thy will be done." That is selflessness. This is what was meant by all the great preachers of ancient times when they taught that God is not the world. What they mean by the world is selfishness. Unselfishness is God. One person may be living on a throne in a golden palace and be perfectly unselfish; then he is in God. Another may live in a hut and wear rags and have nothing in the world; yet if he is selfish, he is an intensely worldly man.

Selfishness Brings On Misery

A CURRENT OF WATER, rushing down of its own nature, falls into a hollow and makes a whirlpool, and after turning around a little there, it emerges again in the form of the free current, to go on unchecked. Each human life is like that current. It becomes involved in this world of space, time, and causation, whirls around a little, crying out, "My father, my mother, my name, my fame," and so on, and at last emerges out of it and regains its original freedom. The whole universe is doing that. Whether we know it or not, whether we are conscious or unconscious of it, we are all working to get out of the dream of the world. The aim of our experience in the world is to enable us to get out of its whirlpool, and Karma Yoga is the knowledge of the secret of this work.

The whole universe is working for salvation, for liberty. From the atom to the highest being, all are working for the one end: liberty of the mind, of the body, of the Spirit. All things are always trying to get freedom, to fly away from bondage. Instead of being knocked about in this universe, we learn from Karma Yoga the secret of work, the method of work, the organizing power of work. A vast mass of energy may be spent in vain if we do not know how to utilize it. Karma Yoga makes a science of work; you learn by it how best to utilize all the activities in this world. Work is inevitable; it must be so. But we should work to the highest purpose. Karma Yoga makes us realize that this world is a world of five minutes, that it is something we have to pass through, and that freedom is only to be found beyond. Karma Yoga shows the process, the secret, and the method of doing work to the best advantage. What does it say? "Work incessantly, but give up all attachment to work."

All that you see, the pains and pleasures and miseries of life, are but the temporary conditions of this world. Poverty and wealth and happiness are but momentary; they do not belong to our real nature at all. Our nature is far beyond misery and happiness, far beyond every object of the senses. And yet we still must work. Misery comes through attachment to the things of the world, not through work. Karma Yoga teaches us how to work without attachment.

The feeling of "I and mine" causes the whole of our misery. With the sense of possession comes selfishness, and selfishness brings on misery. Every act of selfishness or thought of selfishness makes us attached to something, and immediately we are made slaves. Each wave in the mind that says "I and mine" immediately puts a chain around us and makes us slaves; and the more we say "I and mine," the more the slavery grows, and the more the misery increases. Therefore, Karma Yoga tells us to enjoy all the beauty of the world, but not to identify ourselves with any of it. Don't say "mine." Don't say "my house," even in your mind, because when you do, you will forget that all belongs to the Lord, that all *is* the Lord. The whole difficulty is there. Do not project that tentacle of selfishness, "I must possess it." As soon as you do, misery will begin.

So, Karma Yoga says, first destroy the tendency to project this tentacle of selfishness, and when you have the power of checking it, hold it in and do not allow the mind to get into the ways of selfishness. Then you may go out into the world and work as much as you like. Mix everywhere; go where you please; you will never be contaminated by evil. There is the lotus leaf in the water; the water cannot moisten or stick to it; so will you live in the world. This is called *vairagya*, "non-attachment." Non-attachment is the basis of all the yogas. Non-attachment does not mean anything that we may do in relation to our external body; it is all in the mind. The binding link of "me and mine" is in the mind. If we do not have a link with the body or with the things of the senses, we remain non-attached, wherever and whatever we may be. We all must work diligently in order to attain this blissful state of non-attachment. Karma Yoga teaches us the method that will help us in giving up attachment, though it is indeed very hard.

Here are the two ways of giving up all attachment. One way is for those who do not believe in God or in any outside help. They are left simply to work with their own will, with the powers of their mind and discrimination, thinking, "I must be non-attached." However, for those who believe in God, there is another way, which is much less difficult. They offer and dedicate all the fruits of their work to God; they work as worship, and in doing so, they never feel attached to the results. Whatever they see, feel, hear, or do is for God.

Whatever good work we may do, let us not claim any praise for it. It is the Lord's; give up the fruits unto Him. Let us stand aside and know that we are only servants serving God, and that every impulse for action comes from Him every moment. Whatever worship you offer, whatever you do — give all unto Him, and be at rest. Let us all be at perfect peace with ourselves as we give up our selfishness as an eternal sacrifice unto the Lord.

Instead of pouring offerings into the fire, perform this one great sacrifice day and night — the sacrifice of your little self. "I searched for wealth in this world; Thou art the only wealth I have found; I give myself unto Thee." Day and night, let us renounce the selfishness of our seeming self until renunciation becomes a habit with us, until it gets into the blood, the nerves, and the brain, until the whole body is every moment obedient to this idea of selflessness. Go then into the world and its battlefields, and amidst the roaring cannon and the din of war you will find yourself free and at peace.

Looking Upon Work as Worship

EVERY WORK WE DO, every movement of our body, and every thought we think leaves an impression on the mind; and even when these impressions are not obvious on the surface, they are sufficiently strong to work beneath the surface, subconsciously. What we are at every moment is determined by the sum total of these impressions in the mind. What I am just at this moment is the effect of the sum total of all of the impressions of my past. This is really what is meant by character; each person's character is determined by the sum total of these impressions. If good impressions prevail, the character becomes good; if bad impressions prevail, the character becomes bad. If a person continually hears bad words, thinks bad thoughts, does bad deeds, his mind will be full of bad impressions, and they will influence his thought and work without him being conscious of it. These bad impressions are always working, and their result must be evil; and that man will be a bad man; he cannot help it. The sum total of these impressions in him will create a strong motive power for doing bad deeds; he will be like a tool in the hands of his impressions, and they will force him to do evil. Similarly, if a person thinks good thoughts and does good works, the sum total of these impressions will be good; and they, in a similar manner, will force him to do good even in spite of himself. Having done much good work and thought many good thoughts, he has created in himself an irresistible tendency to do good. His mind, controlled by the sum total of his good tendencies, will not then allow him to do evil even if he wishes to do so. The tendencies will turn him back; he is completely under the influence of the good tendencies. When such is the case, a man's good character is said to be established.

The character of a person with control over his motives and sense organs is unchangeably established. He controls his own inner forces, and nothing can draw them out against his will. Through the continuous reflex action of good thoughts and good impressions moving over the surface of the mind, the tendency for doing good becomes very strong, and as a result we are able to control the senses. Thus alone is character established; then alone does a person attain to truth. Such a person is safe forever; he *cannot* do any evil. You may place him in any company; there will be no danger for him.

Freedom of the soul is the goal of all the yogas, and all of them lead to the same result. By work alone we may get to where Buddha or Christ got; the same goal was reached by both of them. The difficulty is that liberation means complete freedom — freedom from the bondage of good as well as from the bondage of evil. A golden chain is as much a chain as an iron one. So the bad tendencies are first to be counteracted by the good ones; the bad impressions in the mind should be removed by fresh waves of good impressions, until all that is evil almost disappears, or is subdued and held in control in a corner of the mind. But after that, our attachment to the good tendencies also has to be conquered. Thus the "attached" will become the "unattached." Work, but let not the action or the thought of it produce a deep impression on the mind. Let the ripples come and go; let huge actions proceed from the muscles and the brain, but let them not make any deep impression on the soul.

Strive to be unattached. Let things work; let the brain centers work, but let not a ripple of selfishness conquer the mind. Work, but do not bind yourself. The whole of nature is for the soul, not the soul for nature. The very reason for nature's existence is the education of the soul; it has no other meaning. It is there because the soul must have knowledge, and through knowledge free itself. If we remember this always, we shall never be attached to nature; we shall know that nature is simply a book that we are to read in order to gain the required knowledge.

Instead of that, however, we identify ourselves with nature; we think that the soul is for nature, that the spirit is for the flesh, and, as the common saying has it, we think that man "lives to eat," and not "eats to live." We are continually making this mistake. We are regarding nature as ourselves and are becoming attached to it; and as soon as this attachment comes, there is the deep impression on the soul, which binds us down and makes us work not from freedom, but like slaves.

Do you not see how everybody works? Ninety-nine percent of us work like slaves, and the result is misery, for it is all selfish work. Selfish work is slave's work. Work through freedom! Work selflessly through love! When we work selfishly as slaves for the things of the world, there can be no love in us, and our work is not real work. Every act of selfless love, however, brings happiness, peace, and blessedness as its reaction. True acts of love can never cause pain, either to the lover or to the beloved.

To attain this level of selflessness is a life's work, but when we reach it we become free; the bondage of nature falls away from us, and we see nature as she is; she forges no more chains for us. Standing entirely free, we take not the rewards of work into consideration. Who then cares what the rewards may be?

So learn to take the position of a giver, in which everything given by you is a free offering to the world, without any thought of return. Then your work will bring you no attachment. Attachment comes only where we expect a return. All thought of obtaining a return for the work we do hinders our spiritual progress, and in the end it brings misery.

If working as a slave results in selfishness and attachment, working as master of our own mind gives rise to the bliss of non-attachment, the bliss of selflessness. There are two things that guide the conduct of people: might and mercy. The exercise of might is invariably the exercise of selfishness. Men and women generally try to make the most of whatever power or advantage they have. Mercy is heaven itself; to be good, we all have to learn to be merciful. Even justice and right should stand on mercy.

There is another way in which this idea of mercy and selfless charity can be put into practice; that is by looking upon work as worship. Here we give all the fruits of our work unto the Lord; and worshiping Him thus, we expect nothing for the work we do. Just as water cannot wet the lotus leaf, so work cannot bind the unselfish man by giving rise to attachment to results. The selfless and unattached man may live in the very heart of a crowded and sinful city, but he will not be touched by sin.

This is what Karma Yoga means: to be of help to everyone, without thought of return, and without asking questions. Never make a vain display of your gifts to the poor, or expect gratitude in return for your service to others, but rather always be grateful to them for giving you the occasion of practicing charity toward them. The true life of spiritual work is such a life of selfless service.

Love, Truth, and Unselfishness

PEOPLE WORK WITH VARIOUS motives; there cannot be work without motive. Some people want to get fame, and so they work for fame. Others want money and they work for money. Some want to have power, and they work for power. Others want to get to heaven, and so they work for that. Others work as penance; they do all sorts of wicked things and then erect a temple or give something to the priests to buy them off and obtain a passport to heaven. They think that this kind of beneficence will clear them and that they will go scot-free in spite of the terrible things they have done. Such are some of the various motives for work.

Now, let us consider work for work's sake. There are some who really are the salt of the earth, who work for work's sake, who do not care for name or fame or even to go to heaven. They work just because good will come of it. There are others who do good to the poor and help humanity from still higher motives, because they believe in doing good and they love good. If a person works without any selfish motive in view, does he not gain something? Yes, he gains the highest benefit. Unselfishness is more paying; only people have not the patience to practice it. Love, truth, and unselfishness are not merely figures of speech used by moralists, but they form our highest ideals, because in them lies such a manifestation of power. In the first place, a person who can work for five days — or even five minutes — without any selfish motive whatsoever, without thinking of the future, of heaven, of punishment, or anything of the kind, has in him or her the capacity to become a powerful moral giant. It is hard to do it, but in our heart of hearts we know its value and the good it brings.

Self-restraint is a manifestation of greater power than any selfish action. All outgoing energy following from a selfish motive is frittered away; it will not cause power to return to you. But if selfishness is restrained, it will result in the development of power. This self-control will tend to produce a mighty will, and a character that makes a Christ or a Buddha.

We have to start from the beginning, to take up works as they come to us and slowly make ourselves more unselfish every day. We must do the work and find out the motive that prompts us; and in the first years we shall find that, almost without exception, our motives are selfish. But gradually this selfishness will melt through persistence, and at last will come the time when we shall be able to do truly unselfish work. We may all hope that someday, as we struggle through the paths of life, there will come a time when we shall become perfectly unselfish; and the moment we attain to that, all our powers will be concentrated, and the glory of our Spirit will be manifest.

Doing Good Is a Blessing to Ourselves

OUR DUTY TO OTHERS means helping others, doing good to the world. Why should we do good to the world? Apparently to help the world, but really to help ourselves. We should always try to help the world. That should be the highest motive in us. We cannot deny that there is much misery in it; to go out and help others, therefore, is the best thing we can do. In the long run, however, we shall find that by helping others we only truly help ourselves.

Each of us manufactures a world for ourselves. Life is good or bad according to the state of mind in which we look at it; it is neither in itself. Fire, in itself, is neither good nor bad. When it keeps us warm we say, "How beautiful fire is!" When it burns our fingers, we curse it. According to how we see it, it produces in us the feeling of good or bad. So also does this world.

While the desire to do good is the highest motive power we have, we must remember that it is a privilege to help others. Do not stand on a high pedestal with money in your hand and say, "Here, my poor man!" Instead, be grateful that the poor man is there, so that by making a gift to him, you are able to help yourself. It is not the receiver that is blessed, but it is the giver. Be thankful that you are allowed to exercise your power of benevolence and mercy in the world, and thus become pure and perfect. All selfless acts help to make us pure and perfect. We must work and constantly do good, because it is a blessing to ourselves. That is the only way we can become perfect. No beggar whom we have helped has ever owed a single cent to us; we owe everything to him, because he has allowed us to exercise our charity on him. Be grateful to those you help. Think of them as manifestations of the Lord. Is it not a great privilege to be allowed to worship God by helping those in need? If we were really unattached, we would escape the pain of any vain expectation of return and could cheerfully do good work in the world. Never will unhappiness or misery come through such selfless work. It is the men and women of great sympathy and love who do good work and so do good to themselves.

We have to bear in mind that we are all debtors to the world, and that the world does not owe us anything. It is a great privilege for all of us to be allowed to do anything for the world. In helping the world, we truly help ourselves. This world will always continue to be a mixture of good and evil. Our duty is to help and sympathize with the weak and to love even the wrongdoer. It is important to always keep in mind that the world is for us a grand moral gymnasium, wherein we are all blessed to be able to take exercise in order to become stronger and stronger spiritually. The result of this exercise is that the more selfless we become, the more shall we love, and the better will be our work.

The Yoga of Unselfish Work

NOTHING IN THE UNIVERSE has power over you until you allow it to exercise such power. Nothing has power over the Spirit of man. By non-attachment you overcome and deny the power of anything to act upon you. The true sign of the person who does not allow anything to work upon him is that good or ill fortune causes no change in his mind; in all conditions he remains in control of his mind.

This very world will become to us a beautiful world when we become masters of our own minds. Nothing will then work upon us as good or evil; we shall find everything to be in its proper place. Often people who begin by saying that the world is a hell end by saying that it is a heaven when they succeed in the practice of self-control.

If we want to be Karma Yogis and train ourselves for the attainment of this state, wherever we may begin we are sure to end in perfect self-abnegation, perfect selflessness. As soon as the little seeming self has gone, the whole world, which at first appears to us to be filled with evil, will appear to be heaven itself, full of blessedness. Its very atmosphere will be blessed. Such is the end and aim of Karma Yoga, and such is its perfection in practical life.

Our various yogas do not conflict with one another; each of them leads us to the same goal and makes us perfect; only each has to be strenuously practiced. The whole secret is in practicing. First you have to hear, then think, and then practice. This is true of every yoga. You have first to hear about it and understand what it is; and many things that you do not understand will be made clear to you by constant hearing and thinking. The external teacher offers only the suggestion, which arouses the internal teacher.

Then things will be made clearer to us by our own power of perception and thought, and we shall realize them in our own souls; and that realization will grow into intense power of will. First it is feeling, then it becomes willing, and out of that willing comes tremendous force for work, until the whole mass of the body is changed into an instrument of the yoga of unselfish work, and the desired result of perfect unselfishness is duly attained.

This attainment does not depend on any dogma or doctrine or belief. Whether you are a Christian or Jew or Hindu, it does not matter. Are you unselfish? That is the question. If you are, you will be perfect without reading a single religious book or going into a single church or temple.

The Law of Life Is Giving

WHATEVER WE DO, we want a return. We are traders in life. And so, if we come to trade, we must abide by the laws of buying and selling. In trading, there are bad times and there are good times; there are rises and falls in prices, and so we must know that blows will inevitably come. However, these blows do not come by what we give, but by what we expect. We get misery for our love, not because we love, but because we want love in return. There is no misery where there is no want. Selfish desires are the source of our misery. These desires, bound by the laws of success and failure, inevitably must bring suffering.

The great secret of true success, then, is this: the person who asks for no return, the perfectly unselfish person, the giving person, is the happiest and the most successful.

Learn to give what you have to give without expectation or demand, and it will come back to you multiplied. But do not think of that as you give; the attention must not be on that. You have the power to give, so give, and there it ends. Learn that the law of life is giving. Nature will force you to give, so give willingly. Sooner or later, you will have to give up everything you own.

We come into life with clenched hands, wanting to take and accumulate. But nature puts a hand on our throat and makes our hands open. Whether you want to or not, you have to give. The moment you say, "I will not," a blow comes, and you are hurt. All of us will be compelled, in the long run, to give up all of our possessions, and the more one struggles against this law, the more miserable one feels. It is only because we dare not give freely that we are miserable, because we are not yet willing enough to accede to this grand demand of nature.

Therefore, learn to give cheerfully, seeking nothing in return; as a result, the more you give, the more will come to you. The more quickly you empty the air out of this room, the more quickly it will be filled up by external air. But if you close all the doors and every window, that which is within will remain, and that which is outside will never come in, causing what is within to stagnate, degenerate, and become poisoned. A river is continually emptying itself into the ocean and is continually filling up again. Bar not the exit into the ocean. The moment you do that, death seizes you. Therefore, be not the taker. Every day, renew your determination to be the giver.

The Great Secret of Karma Yoga

THE BHAGAVAD GITA TEACHES Karma Yoga, the power of work through concentration. In such concentration in action, there is no consciousness of the lower ego present. The consciousness that I am doing this and that is never present when one works through Yoga. The Western people do not understand this. They say that if there is no consciousness of ego, if this ego is gone, how then can a person work? But when one works with concentration, losing all consciousness of oneself, the work that is done is infinitely better, and this is a fact that everyone has experienced in his or her own life. There are some works that we perform by becoming so immersed in them that there is no experience of ego whatsoever.

If the painter, losing the consciousness of his ego, becomes completely immersed in his painting, he will be able to produce great work. If the cook concentrates his whole self on the food he handles, he will lose all other consciousness for the time being. But even in these examples, they are only able to do perfectly in this way a single work to which they have become habituated. The Bhagavad Gita teaches that *all* works should be done thus. Those who are one with the Lord through Yoga perform all their works immersed in concentration and completely detached from ego, and, as such, have no thought of themselves or personal benefit. Such a performance of work brings only good to the world.

Those who work without any consciousness of their ego are not affected by evil, for they work for the welfare of the world. To work in service, unattached to ego and without personal motive in mind, brings the highest bliss and freedom. This is the great secret of Karma Yoga taught by Lord Krishna in the Bhagavad Gita.

Out of Purity Comes True Power

OUR BEST WORK IS DONE, our greatest influence is exerted, when we are without thought of self. All great geniuses know this. Let us open ourselves to the one Divine Actor, and let Him act through us. Be perfectly unfocused upon yourself; then alone will you do true work. Put out self, lose it, forget it; just let God work through you. It is His business. We have nothing to do but stand aside and let God work. The more we go away, the more God comes in. Get rid of the little "I," and let only the great "I" live through you.

We are what our thoughts have made us; so take care what you think. Thoughts live; they travel far. Desire nothing selfishly; give, think of God, and look for no return. It is the selfless who bring results. As soon as we say "I," we are bound. The Lord has hidden Himself best, and His work is best; so he who hides himself best, accomplishes most. Conquer *yourself,* and the whole universe is yours.

In the state of spiritual illumination we see the very nature of things, we go beyond the senses and beyond reason. The unyielding wall that shuts us in is egoism, always referring everything to ourselves, thinking, "I do this, that, and the other." Get rid of this puny "I," so full of self-will and so blind to the Spirit; renounce this darkness in us. "Not I, but Thou" — say it, feel it, live it. Until we give up the world manufactured by the ego, never can we enter the kingdom of heaven. None ever did, none ever will. To give up selfishness is to forget the ego, to know it not at all — living *in* the body, but not *of* it. This rascal ego must be obliterated.

Selfish desire is the million-headed serpent that we have to tread under foot. We must renounce it and move beyond it. The world of the senses is a kingdom of which the puny ego is king.

Put it away and stand firm. Hold fast to the Lord, and at last you shall reach a state of perfection. Know that any idea that the gratification of the senses constitutes true joy is purely illusory. There is not one spark of real joy there; all the joy there is, is a mere reflection of the true bliss of the Spirit.

Out of purity comes true power. One person purified thoroughly accomplishes more than a regiment of preachers. The real power in the world is with the pure ones, those who only live to love. They never say "me and mine"; they are simply blessed in being instruments of the Lord. Such men and women, ever living fully identified with God and asking nothing, are ideal existences. They are the real movers, the ever-free, the absolutely selfless. With their little personalities entirely blown away, all that remains is the Lord. Such people are the makers of Christs and Buddhas.

Bhakti Yoga

Oneness through Selfless Love

Swami Vivekananda, Alameda, California, 1900

Bhakti Yoga

BHAKTI YOGA IS FOR the person of emotional nature, the lover. This person wants to love God, and he relies upon and uses all sorts of rituals, flowers, incense, beautiful buildings, forms, and all such things. It is good for you to remember, especially in this country, that the world's great spiritual giants have all been produced by those religious sects that have been in possession of very rich mythology and ritual. Therefore, do not decry these rituals and mythologies. The greatest people I have seen in my life, the most wonderfully developed in spirituality, have all come through the discipline of these rituals. So let people have all the mythology they want, with its beautiful inspirations; for you must always bear in mind that emotional natures do not care for abstract definitions of truth. God to them is something tangible. To the Bhakta, He is the only thing that is real; and they feel Him, they hear Him, they see Him, and, of course, they love Him.

Bhakti Yoga teaches how to love without any ulterior motive, loving God and loving goodness because it is good to do so: not for going to heaven, or to get wealth or anything else. It teaches that love itself is the highest recompense of love — that God Himself *is* love. The highest idea that the human mind can conceive of Him is that He is the God of Love. "Wherever there is love, it is He, the Lord, present there." Where the husband kisses the wife, He is there in the kiss; where the mother kisses the child, He is there in the kiss; where friends clasp hands, He, the Lord, is present as the God of Love. Whenever we love or help anyone in need, God is there, giving freely His bounty out of His love for humanity. Wherever the heart expands, God is there manifested. This is what Bhakti Yoga teaches.

The Lord Is the Great Magnet

BHAKTI YOGA IS THE SCIENCE of higher love. It shows us how to direct love: how to manage it, how to use it, how to give it a new aim; and from it, how to obtain the highest and most glorious results; that is, how to make it lead us to spiritual blessedness. Bhakti Yoga does not say, "Give up"; it says only, "Love the Highest!" and everything low will naturally fall away from him or her, the object of whose love is this Highest.

What is really required of us in this yoga is that our thirst after the beautiful should be directed to God. What is the beauty in the human face, in the sky, in the stars, and in the moon? It is only the partial manifestation of the real, all-embracing Divine Beauty. "He shining, everything shines. It is through His light that all things shine." Take this high position of Bhakti, which makes you forget at once all your little personalities.

Take yourself away from all of the world's selfish little clingings. Stand as a witness, and observe and study the phenomena of nature. You will be able to see that there are millions and millions of channels through which God is manifesting Himself as Love.

"Wherever there is any bliss, even if it is of the most sensual kind, there is a spark of that Eternal Bliss that is the Lord Himself." Even in the lowest kinds of attraction there is the germ of divine love.

One of the names of the Lord, in Sanskrit, is Hari, and this means "He who attracts all things to Himself." His is, in fact, the only attraction felt by human hearts. Who can really attract a soul? Only God. Do you think dead matter can truly attract the soul? It never did and never will. When you see a man going after a beautiful face, do you think it is the handful of arranged material molecules that really attracts the man? Not at all. Behind those material particles there must be and is the play of divine influence and divine love. The ignorant man does not know it; but yet, consciously or unconsciously, he is attracted by it and it alone.

All forms of attraction derive their power from God Himself. "None, O beloved, ever loved the husband for the husband's sake; it is the Atman, the Lord who is within the husband, that is loved. None, O beloved, ever loved the wife for the wife's sake; it is the Atman, the Lord who is within the wife, that is loved." Loving husbands and wives may or may not know this, but it is true all the same. Similarly, no one loves a child, or anything else in the world, but for the sake of Him who is within.

The Lord is the great magnet, and we are all like iron filings; we are being constantly attracted by Him, and all of us are struggling to reach Him. All this struggling of ours in this world is surely not intended for selfish ends. The work of our lives is, after all, to approach the great magnet. All the tremendous struggling and fighting in life is intended to help us ultimately go to Him and be one with Him.

The Bhakti Yogi knows the meaning of life's struggles; she understands it. She wants to go directly to the center of all attraction, the Blessed Lord. This is the renunciation of the Bhakta. This mighty attraction in the direction of God makes all lesser attractions vanish for her. This mighty Infinite Love of God that enters her heart leaves no place for any lesser loves to live there. How could it be otherwise? Bhakti fills her heart with the divine waters of the ocean of love, which is God Himself; there is no place there for selfish little loves.

This is the ideal preparation for the attainment of the supreme Bhakti. When this renunciation comes, the gate opens for the soul to pass through, and the lofty regions of supreme devotion, or Para-Bhakti, are reached. She has attained that supreme state of love. She sees no distinctions; the mighty ocean of love has entered into her, and she sees not man in man, but beholds her Beloved everywhere. Through every face shines to her the Beloved. The light in the sun or the moon is all His manifestation. Wherever there is beauty or sublimity, to her it is all His.

Loving the Universal

HOW CAN WE LOVE the particular without first loving the universal? God is the universal whole; and the universe that we see is the particularized entity. To truly love the things of the material universe is possible only by way of loving the universal. The search after the universal is the one search of Indian philosophy and religion. The Jnani aims at the wholeness of things, at that one absolute and generalized Being which by knowing he knows everything. The Bhakta, on the other hand, wishes to realize that one generalized abstract Being, which by loving he loves the whole universe.

The conclusion to which the Bhakta comes is that if you go on merely loving one person after another, you may go on loving them for an infinite length of time without being in the least able to love the world as a whole. However, when at last one arrives at the central idea that all love is God, and that the sum total of the aspirations of all the souls in the universe, whether they be free or bound or struggling toward liberation, is also God, then alone does it become possible for one to manifest universal love.

God is the universal, and this visible universe is God differentiated and made manifest. If we love God, we love everything. Loving the world and doing good to it will all come easily then. But we have to obtain this power by loving God first; otherwise, it is no easy matter to do good to the world.

"Everything is His and He is my Lover. I love Him," says the Bhakta. In this way, everything becomes sacred to the Bhakta, because all things are His. All are His children, His body, His manifestation. How then can we hurt anyone? How then can we dislike anyone? With love of God will come, as a sure effect, love for everyone in the universe. The nearer we approach God, the more do we begin to see that all things are in Him.

When the soul succeeds in enjoying the bliss of this supreme love, it also begins to see Him in everything. Our heart thus becomes an eternal fountain of love. And when we reach even higher states of this love, all the little differences between the things of the world are entirely lost. A man or woman is seen no more as a human being, but as God; an animal is seen no more as an animal, but as a manifestation of God. Thus, in this intense state of Bhakti, worship is offered to everyone — to every life and to every being. "Knowing that the Lord is in every being, the wise have thus to manifest unswerving love toward all beings." As a result of this kind of intense, all-absorbing love comes the feeling of perfect self-surrender, the conviction that nothing that happens is against us. The realization of such an ideal, in which the sense of little self is completely lost, is the very pinnacle of the religion of love.

The Lord Speaks through the Heart

WHEN THERE IS CONFLICT between the heart and the brain, let the heart be followed, because intellect has only one state, reason, and only within reason does intellect work; it cannot get beyond it. It is the heart that takes one to the highest plane, which intellect can never reach; it goes beyond intellect, and reaches to what is called inspiration. Intellect can never become inspired; only the heart, when it is enlightened, becomes inspired. An intellectual but heartless person never becomes an inspired person. It is always the heart that speaks in the man or woman of love; it discovers a greater instrument than the intellect can give you, the instrument of inspiration. Just as the intellect is the instrument of knowledge, so is the heart the instrument of inspiration. However, in a lower state, the heart is a much weaker instrument than the intellect. An ignorant person knows nothing, for he lives in the lower emotions. Compare him with a great professor, and you can see what wonderful power the latter possesses! And yet the professor, bound by his intellect, can be an intellectual man *and* the devil at the same time, while the man or woman of true heart can never be a devil. Properly cultivated, the heart will be elevated, and will go beyond intellect; there, it will be changed into inspiration. Everyone will go beyond intellect in the end.

There are preparations for the heart, for that love, for that intense sympathy pertaining to the heart. It is not at all necessary to be educated or learned to get to God; it is only necessary that you are pure. If you are pure, you will reach God. "Blessed are the pure in heart, for they shall see God."

If you are not pure, and you know all the sciences in the world, that will not help you at all; you may be buried in all the books you read, but that will not be of much use. It is the pure heart that reaches the goal. A pure heart sees beyond the intellect; it knows things that reason can never know. Whenever there is conflict between the pure heart and the intellect, always side with the pure heart, even if you think what your heart is doing is unreasonable.

When it is desirous of doing good to others, your mind may tell you that it is not politic to do so, but follow your heart's desire to do good, and you will find that you make fewer mistakes than by following your intellect. The pure heart is the best mirror for the reflection of truth, so all these disciplines are for the purification of the heart. And as soon as it is pure, all truths flash upon it in an instant; all truth in the universe will manifest in your heart, if you are sufficiently pure.

The great truths about atoms and the finer elements were discovered ages ago by people who never saw a telescope or a microscope or a laboratory. How did they know all these things? It was through the heart; they purified the heart. It is open to us, and even necessary for us to do the same today, for it is the cultivation of the heart, and not of the intellect, that will lessen the misery of the world.

Intellect has been cultivated, with the result that hundreds of sciences have been discovered, and their effect has been that the few have made slaves of the many. Artificial wants have been created; and every person, whether he has money or not, desires to have those wants satisfied, and when he cannot, he struggles and dies in the struggle. This is the result. Through the intellect is not the way to solve the problem of misery, but through the heart. If all this vast amount of effort had been spent in making people purer, gentler, and more forbearing, this world would have a thousand-fold more happiness than it has today. So always cultivate the heart, for only through the heart does the Lord speak.

Ishvara, the Personal God

WHO IS ISHVARA, the Personal God? He is "the Eternal, the Pure, the Ever-Free, the Almighty, the All-Knowing, the All-Merciful." "From Ishvara comes the birth, continuation, and dissolution of the universe." "He, the Lord of the universe, is, of His own nature, inexpressible Love." These are some of the definitions of Ishvara, the Personal God.

Are there then two Gods; Brahman, the absolute Existence-Knowledge-Bliss of the philosopher, and this God of Love of the Bhakta? No; it is the one Infinite who is also the God of Love; the impersonal and the personal are one.

It has always to be understood that the Personal God worshiped by the Bhakta is not separate or different from Brahman. All is Brahman, the One without a second; but Brahman, as unity or absolute, is too much of an abstraction to be loved, so the Bhakta chooses to worship the relative aspect of Brahman, which is Ishvara, the Personal God, the supreme Creator, Sustainer, and Dissolver of the universe. To use a simile: Brahman is like the clay, or the substance out of which an infinite variety of articles are fashioned. As clay, they are all one; but form, or manifestation, differentiates them. Before every one of them was made, they all existed as clay, identical substantially; but when formed, and so long as the form remains, they are separate and different. The clay mouse can never become a clay elephant, because, as manifestations, it is form alone that makes them what they are. As unformed clay, they are all one. All things in the universe are Brahman in manifestation and form, and Ishvara, the Personal God, is the highest manifestation of the Absolute Reality, or, in other words, the highest possible reading of the Absolute by the human mind.

Preparatory Bhakti

THE BEST DEFINITION OF Bhakti Yoga is perhaps this prayer: "That abiding love that the non-discriminating have for the fleeting objects of the senses, may I have the same sort of love for Thee." We see what a strong love those who do not know any better have for sense objects, for money, for fame, and for possessions — what a tremendous clinging they have to all these things! This love, when given to God, is called Bhakti. Bhakti is not destructive; it teaches us that none of the faculties we have has been given in vain, that the natural way to come to liberation is *through* them. Bhakti does not restrain anything, it does not go against nature; it only gives it a higher and more powerful direction. When the same kind of love that has before been given to sense-objects is given to God, it is called Bhakti.

We must not be extremely attached to anything except God. See everything, do everything, but be not attached. As soon as extreme attachment comes, a man loses himself; he is no more master of himself, he is a slave. If a woman is extremely attached to a man, she becomes a slave to that man, or the man to the woman. There is no use in being a slave. There are higher things in this world than becoming a slave to a human being. Love and do good to everybody, but do not become a slave. It only degenerates us and makes us extremely selfish. A good many of the wicked deeds done in this world are done because of this extreme attachment to people and things. So, barring attachment to good works, all attachment that enslaves should be avoided, and love should be given freely to everybody.

When the senses, without being attached, work in the world, such work is called "pure food." When the food is pure, the mind is able to take in objects and think about them without attachment, jealousy, or delusion; then the mind becomes pure, and when that is the case, constant remembrance of God is in that mind.

This world is good so far as it is a means to purify and perfect ourselves, and as soon as it has ceased to be that, it becomes a means of greater bondage. So money and learning are good so long as they help us go forward; but as soon as they have ceased to do that, they only bring greater ignorance and misery. If money or learning helps a person to do good to others, they are of value; but if not, they are simply a means of greater selfishness, and the sooner they are gotten rid of, the better.

The mind should always be directed toward God; nothing should have any right to withhold it. We should continuously think of the love of God, although this is a very hard task; yet it can be done by persistent practice. What we are now is the result of past practice, and practice will make us what we shall be. Thinking of the senses has brought us down here to live a moment, to cry a moment, and to be at the mercy of every breeze, slave to everything.

Go the other way; let the mind think of God alone. When it tries to think of anything else, give it a good blow, so that it may turn around and remember God again. We should not only impose this practice on the mind, but the senses, too, should be employed. Instead of hearing foolish things, we should hear about God; instead of talking foolish words, we should talk of God; and instead of reading foolish books, we should read books that tell of the glory of God.

Always bear in mind that the memory of God will not come to the selfish person. The more we come out and do good to others, the more our hearts will be purified and God will be in them. The first of everything should go to the poor, for they are God's representatives; everyone that suffers is His representative. The person who lives without giving, and enjoys life so, lives in ignorance.

The lowest man is the one whose hands draw in, in taking. The highest man is the one whose hands go out, in giving. Remember that the hands were made for that, to give always.

The Bhakta's Love

WHEN THE HIGHEST IDEAL of the Bhakta's love of God is reached, philosophy is thrown away; who then will want for it? Freedom, Salvation, Nirvana — all are thrown away; who cares to become free while living in the enjoyment of Divine Love? "Lord, I do not care for wealth, nor beauty, nor learning, nor even freedom; let me be born again and again, and be Thou ever my Love. Be Thou ever and ever my Love." "Who cares to become sugar?" says the Bhakta; "I want to taste sugar." Who will then desire to become free and one with God? "I may know that I am He; yet will I take myself away from Him and become different, so that I may enjoy the divine sweetness of the Beloved." That is what the Bhakta says. Love for love's sake is his highest joy.

A Bhakta cares for nothing but love, to love and to be loved. His unworldly love is a burning madness before which everything else vanishes for him. The whole universe is to him full of love and love alone; that is how it seems to the lover. So when a man has this love in him, he becomes eternally blessed, eternally happy. He has drawn near to God, and in doing so he has thrown off all those vain desires of which he was full before. This blessed madness of divine love cures forever the disease of selfishness that is in us.

We all have to begin as dualists in the religion of love. God is to us a separate Being, and we feel ourselves to be separate beings also. Love then comes in the middle, and we begin to approach God, and God also comes nearer and nearer to us. We take up all the various relationships of life, as son or daughter, as mother or father, as friend, as lover, and so on, and we project them on our ideal of love, on our God. To us, God exists as all these, and the last point of our progress is reached when we become absolutely merged with the object of our worship. We all begin with love for ourselves, and the unfair claims of the little self make even love selfish. At last, however, comes the full blaze of light, in which this little self is seen to have become one with the Infinite. We ourselves are transfigured in the presence of this Light of Love, and we realize at last the beautiful and inspiring truth that Love, the Lover, and the Beloved, are One.

God Is the Highest Goal

IN THE WESTERN COUNTRIES, as a rule, people put more stress on the body aspect of the human being. However, the philosophers in India who wrote on Bhakti put greater stress on the spiritual side of the human being; and this difference seems to be typical of the Eastern and Western nations. It is so even in common language. In England, when speaking of death, you say a man gives up his spirit; in India, a man gives up his body. The one idea is that man is a body and has a soul, the other that man is a soul and has a body. Those whose idea is that man is a body and has a soul put all the stress on the body. If you ask such a person why he lives, you will be told that it is to enjoy life; to enjoy the senses, to enjoy possessions, to enjoy the things of the world. He cannot dream of anything beyond even if he is told of it; his idea of an afterlife is but a heightened continuation of this enjoyment. He thinks that when he dies he will go to some place where he will have the same enjoyments, the same senses, only in strengthened forms. He worships God, believing that God is the means to attain this end. The goal of his life is enjoyment of sense-objects, and he has come to believe that there is a Being who will give him a very long lease on these enjoyments, and with this idea he worships God.

On the other hand, the Indian idea is that God is the supreme goal of life; that there is nothing beyond God, and that these sense-enjoyments are simply something through which we are now passing in the hope of realizing higher things. Not only so, but that it would be disastrous and terrible if people had nothing to look forward to but sense-enjoyments. In our everyday lives, we find that the less the sense-enjoyments, the higher the life of the man. And the lower the man, the more delight he finds in the senses. As he gets higher, reason and love become the goal of his life. In proportion to the development of these faculties, he loses interest in the mere enjoyment of the senses.

If we take for granted that a certain amount of power is given to us, and that it can be spent either on the body, or on the mind, or on the Spirit, then all the power spent on any one of these leaves just so much less to be expended on the others. We see then that if we desire only to have nice sense-enjoyments all the time, we shall necessarily inhibit our spiritual growth. A man does not know what harm he is asking for when he says he only wants to go to a place where his sense-enjoyments will be intensified. Observe the pig as he eats; it is his heaven, and if the greatest angel came and looked on, the pig would not even look up; his whole existence is in eating.

So with people desiring a heaven full of sense-pleasures. They are like the pig, wallowing in the mire of the senses, unable to see anything beyond. Their sense-enjoyment is all that they want, and the loss of it is the loss of heaven to them. In this lowly condition, people like these can never be Bhaktas, true lovers of God.

However, even if this lower ideal is followed for a time, it will in the course of time change; each of us will eventually find that there is something higher, of which we did not know, and our clinging to life and to things of the senses will gradually fall away. Each one of us has an ideal of heaven just as we want it to be, but as we grow in wisdom and see higher things, we will catch higher glimpses beyond. And what can be higher than God? God Himself is the highest goal of humanity, and to see Him and serve Him is the highest heaven on earth.

Love Is Always the Highest Ideal

LOVE WE HEAR SPOKEN of everywhere. The world is full of the talk of love, but it is hard to love. Where is love? How do you know that there is love? The first test of love is that it knows no bargaining. So long as you see a person love another to get something, you may know that it is not true love; it is shopkeeping. Wherever there is any question of buying and selling, it is not love. So when we pray to God, "Give me this and give that," it is not love. How can it be? I offer you a prayer and you give me something in return; that is what it is, mere shopkeeping.

What is the difference between love and shopkeeping? Love is always the giver, and never the taker. The nature of real love is that it does not ask for anything in return. The Bhakta loves God because He is lovable; there is no other motive originating or directing this divine emotion of the true devotee. Says the child of God, "If God wants, I give Him my everything, because I love Him; and because I want to love Him, I ask no favor in return. Sufficient for me that He is the God of love. I ask no more questions."

The second test is that love knows no fear. How can there be any fright in love? Does the lamb love the lion? Does the mouse love the cat? Does the slave love the master? Slaves sometimes simulate love, but is it love? Where do you ever see love in fear? It is always a sham. So long as we think of God as sitting above the clouds, with a reward in one hand and punishment in the other, there can be no love. With love never comes the idea of fear or of anything that makes us afraid. The children of God never see Him as a punisher or rewarder. Only people who have never tasted of the love of God fear Him and quake all their lives before Him. Cast off all these fearful ideas of God as a punisher or rewarder.

Some men and women, even the most intellectual, are spiritual beginners, and these ideas may help them. But to those in whom spiritual insight is awakened, such ideas are simply foolish. Such people reject all ideas of fear, because they know that love is the highest ideal. When one has passed through the first two stages, when one has thrown off all shopkeeping and cast off all fear, only then does one begin to realize that love is always the highest ideal.

The Light of Love

WHAT IS THE IDEAL of the lover of God who has quite passed beyond the idea of selfishness, of bartering and bargaining, and who knows no fear in his love of God? When a person has acquired this conviction, his ideal becomes one of perfect love, one of perfect fearlessness born of love. The highest ideal of such a person has no narrowness of particularity about it; it is love universal, love without limits and bonds, love itself, love absolute.

When the devotee has reached this point, he is no longer impelled to ask whether God can be demonstrated or not, whether He is omnipotent and omniscient or not. To him, He is the God of Love, the highest ideal of love, and that is sufficient for all his purposes. He, as love, is self-evident; no proofs are required to demonstrate the existence of the Beloved to the lover. The magistrate Gods of other forms of religion may require a good deal of proof to prove them, but the lover of God does not and cannot think of such Gods at all. To him, God exists entirely as love. "None, O beloved, loves the husband for the husband's sake; it is for the sake of the Lord who is in the husband that the husband is loved. None, O beloved, loves the wife for the wife's sake; it is for the sake of the Lord who is in the wife that the wife is loved."

When I think of myself as comprehending the Universal, there can surely be no selfishness in me; but when, by mistake, I think that I am something little, my love becomes particularized and narrowed. The mistake consists in making the sphere of love narrow and contracted. All things in the universe are of divine origin and deserve to be loved. The love of the whole includes the love of the parts.

This whole is the God of the Bhaktas, and all the other ideas of God; Fathers in Heaven, Rulers or Creators, theories and doctrines and books, have no purpose and no meaning for them, seeing that they have through their supreme love and devotion risen above those things altogether. When the heart is purified and cleansed and filled to the brim with the divine nectar of love, all other ideas of God become simply puerile and are rejected as being inadequate or unworthy. Such is indeed the power of Supreme Love. The perfected Bhakta no longer goes to see God in temples and churches; he knows no place where he will not find Him. He finds Him outside the temple as well as in the temple. He finds Him in the saint, and he find Him even in the wicked, because he has Him already seated in glory in his own heart as the one Almighty, inextinguishable Light of Love, which is ever shining and eternally present everywhere.

Shining in Everything Is Love

THIS EXTERNAL WORLD IS only the world of suggestion. All that we see, we project out of our own minds. External things furnish us with suggestions, over which we project out our own ideals and make our objects. The wicked see this world as a perfect hell, and the good see it as a perfect heaven. Lovers see this world as full of love, and haters see it as full of hatred. Fighters see nothing but strife, and the peaceful see nothing but peace; the perfected man or woman, however, sees nothing but God.

When we have reached the point where we love the ideal as the ideal, all arguments and doubts vanish forever. Who cares whether a God can be demonstrated or not? Who cares whether God can be almighty and all-merciful at the same time or not? Who cares whether He is the rewarder of humanity or whether He looks at us with the eyes of a tyrant or with the eyes of a beneficent monarch?

The true lover of God has passed beyond all these things — beyond rewards and punishments, beyond fears or doubts, beyond scientific or any other demonstration. Sufficient unto him is the ideal of love, and is it not self-evident that this universe is but a manifestation of this love? What is it that makes atoms join with atoms and molecules with molecules, that sets big planets flying toward each other, that attracts man to woman, woman to man, human beings to human beings, and animals to animals, that draws the whole universe, as it were, toward one center? It is love. Its manifestation is evident, from the lowest atom to the highest being: omnipresent, all-pervading is this love. What manifests itself as attraction in the sentient and the insentient, in the particular and in the universal, is the love of God. It is the one motive power in the universe. Under the impetus of that love, Christ gives his life for humanity, the mother gives her life for the child, and the husband gives his life for the wife. It is under the impetus of the same love that people are ready to give up their lives for their country, and, strange to say, it is under the impetus of that same love that the thief goes to steal. Love is the one motive power in the universe. The thief has love for gold; the love is there, but it is misdirected. So, in all crimes as well as in all virtuous actions, behind them all stands that eternal love. Suppose one person writes a check for a thousand dollars for the poor of New York, and at the same time, in the same room, another person forges the name of a friend. The light by which both of them write is the same, but each one is responsible for the use he makes of it. It is not the light that is to be blamed or praised. Unattached, yet shining in everything, is love, the motive power of the universe, without which the universe would fall to pieces in a moment, and this infinite love is God.

The Peace of the Bhakta

WE MAY ALL MANAGE to maintain our bodies, more or less satisfactorily, for a longer interval of time. Nevertheless, our bodies will eventually have to go, for there is no permanence about them. And so blessed are they whose bodies are given in the service of others. In this material world, there being one thing certain, namely, death, it is far better that this body dies in a good cause than in a bad one. "In this evanescent world, where everything eventually falls to pieces, we have to make the highest use of what we have," says the Bhakta; and really the highest use of life is to hold it at the service of all beings.

To the vast majority of human beings, the body is everything; bodily enjoyment is their all in all. It is the delusion that we are wholly the body we own that breeds all the selfishness in the world, that causes us to constantly, and by all possible means, try so hard to please it. If you know that you are Spirit and not the body, then you have none to fight with or struggle against; you are dead to all ideas of selfishness.

To those who have experienced it, this eternal sacrifice of the little self unto the beloved Lord is higher by far than all wealth and power, even than all soaring thoughts of renown and enjoyment. The peace of the Bhakta is a peace that passeth all understanding and is of incomparable value. In this state everything in the shape of attachment goes away, except that one all-absorbing love for Him in whom all things live and move and have their being. This attachment of love for God is indeed the one attachment that does not bind the soul, but effectively breaks all of its bondages.

Serve the Highest Ideal

THE WORLD MAY BE said to be divided between persons of lower nature, who think that the gratification of the body is the end-all and be-all of existence, and persons of godly nature, who realize that the body is simply a means to an end, an instrument intended for the culture of the soul.

In Bhakti Yoga, the central secret is to know that the various passions and feelings and emotions in the human heart are not wrong in themselves; they only have to be carefully controlled and given a higher and higher direction, until they attain the very highest condition of excellence. The highest direction is that which takes us to God; every other direction is lower. We find that pleasures and pains are very common and oft-recurring feelings in our lives. When a person feels pain because he has not wealth or some such worldly thing, he is giving a wrong direction to the feeling. Let him feel pain that he has not reached the Highest, that he has not yet reached the Light of God, and then that pain will eventually lead to his illumination and salvation. When you become glad because you have a handful of coins, it is a wrong direction given to the faculty of joy; it should be given a higher direction, it must be made to serve the Highest Ideal. Pleasure in the Highest Ideal must surely be our greatest joy. This same thing is true of all our other feelings. The Bhakta says that not one of our feelings is wrong; he takes hold of them all and points them unfailingly toward God.

The Theory of Ishta

THE THEORY OF ISHTA is a subject requiring careful attention, because with a proper understanding of it, all the various religions of the world can be understood. The word Ishta is derived from the root word *ish*, "to desire; to choose." The ideal of all religions, all sects, is the same — the attaining of liberty and the cessation of misery. Wherever you find religion, you will find this ideal working in one form or another. Of course, in lower stages of religion it is not so well expressed; but still, well or ill expressed, it is the goal to which every religion approaches. All of us want to be free of suffering; we are all struggling to attain to freedom — physical, mental, and spiritual. This is the whole idea upon which the world is working. Though the goal is one and the same, there may be many ways to reach it; and these ways are determined by the peculiarities of our nature. One person's nature is emotional, another's intellectual, another's active, and so on. And even in the same nature there may be many subdivisions. Take, for instance, love, with which we are specially concerned in this subject of Bhakti Yoga. One person's nature has a stronger love for children; another has it for husband or wife, another for mother, another for father, another for friends, another for country, and a few for humanity in the broadest sense.

We find that even in one subject there are so many different ways of attaining to its goal. All Christians believe in Christ; but think how many different explanations they have of him. Each church sees him in a different light, from different standpoints. The Presbyterian's eyes are fixed upon that scene in Christ's life when he went to the money changers; he looks on him as a fighter. If you ask a Quaker, perhaps he will say, "He forgave his enemies."

The Quaker takes that view, and so on. If you ask a Roman Catholic what point of Christ's life is the most pleasing to him, he perhaps will say, "When he gave the keys to Peter." Each sect is bound to see him in its own way.

It follows that there will be many divisions and subdivisions even of the same subject. Small-minded people take one of these subdivisions and take their stand upon it, and they not only deny the right of every other person to interpret the universe according to his or her own light, but dare to say that others are entirely wrong, and they alone are right. But what is the position taken in Bhakti Yoga? Not only that we would not tell others that they are wrong, but that we would tell them that they are right — all of these who sincerely follow their own ways. That way which your nature makes it absolutely necessary for you to take is the right way for you. Each one of us is born with a peculiarity of nature as the result of our past existence. Either we call it our reincarnated past experience or our hereditary past; whatever way we may put it, we are the result of the past — that is absolutely certain, through whatever channels that past may have come. It naturally follows that each one of us is an effect, of which our past has been the cause; and as such, there is a peculiar movement, a peculiar train in each one of us; and therefore we will all have to find our own way.

This way, this method, to which each of us is naturally adapted, is called the chosen way. This is the theory of Ishta, and the way that is ours we call our own Ishta. For instance, one person's idea of God is that He is the omnipotent ruler of the universe. He may be an overbearing man who wants to rule everyone; he naturally finds God an omnipotent ruler. Another person, perhaps a schoolmaster and severe, cannot see any other God but a God of justice and punishment. Still another person, kindly and loving, sees God as the benevolent and merciful Father, and so on. Each one sees God according to his or her own nature; and this vision, conditioned by our own nature, is our Ishta. We have brought ourselves to a position where we can see that vision of God, and that alone; we cannot see any other vision.

To explain it a little further, we must understand that truth seen from different standpoints can still be truth, and yet not the same truth. This would seem at first to be a contradiction in terms, but we must remember that an absolute truth is only one, while relative truths are necessarily various. Take your vision of the sun, for instance. The sun is one; but when you and I and a hundred other people stand at different places and look at it, each one of us sees a different sun. We cannot help it. A very little change of place will change a person's whole vision of the sun. A slight change in the atmosphere will make again a different vision. So, in relative perception, truth always appears various. But Absolute Truth is only one. Therefore, we need not fight with others when we find that they are saying something about religion that is not exactly according to our view of it. We ought to remember that both views may be true, even if apparently contradictory.

There may be millions of radii converging toward the same center in the sun. The farther they are from the center, the greater is the distance between any two. But as they all meet at the center, all difference vanishes. There is such a center, which is the absolute goal of humanity. It is God. We are the radii. The distances between the radii are the constitutional limitations through which we alone can catch the vision of God. While standing on this plane, each one of us is bound to have a different view of the Absolute Reality; and as such, all views are true, and no one of us need quarrel with another. The only solution lies in approaching the center. If we try to settle our differences by argument or quarreling, we shall find that we can go on for thousands of years without coming to a conclusion. History proves that. The only solution is to march ahead toward the center, toward God, and the sooner we do that, the sooner our differences will vanish.

Love God the Way You Love Best

AND SO THIS THEORY of Ishta really means allowing a person to choose his or her own religion. No man has the right to force another to worship what he worships. All attempts to herd together human beings by means of armies, force, or arguments, to drive them pell-mell into the same enclosure and make them worship the same God have failed, and will fail always, because it is constitutionally impossible to do so. Not only that, there is the danger of arresting their growth.

You cannot make a plant grow in soil unsuited to it. But you can *help* it to go forward in its own way by taking away the obstacles so that the necessary knowledge can come out of its own nature. Loosen the soil a little, so that it may come out easily. Put a hedge around it; see that it is not harmed by anything, and there your work stops. You cannot do anything else. The rest is a manifestation from *within* its own nature.

The same is true here: You come to listen to me, and when you go home and compare what you have learned, you will find that you have thought out the same things; I have only given them expression. I cannot teach you anything: you will have to teach yourself. But I can perhaps help you in giving expression to your thoughts.

So in religion — more so — I must teach myself religion. What right has my mother or father to put all sorts of nonsense into my head? What right have my teachers or society to put things into my head? Perhaps they are good for others, but they may not be good for me; they may not be my way. Think of the appalling evil that is in the world today, of the millions and millions of innocent children perverted by wrong ways of teaching. How many beautiful things that would have become wonderful spiritual truths have been nipped in the bud by this terrible idea of a family religion, a social religion, a national religion, and so on. Think of what a mass of superstition is in your head just now about the religion of your childhood or the religion of your country!

There are so many ideals; I have no right to say what shall be your ideal, or to force any ideal upon you. My duty should be to lay before you all the ideals I know of, and enable you to see by your own constitution which you like best, and which is most fitted to you. Take up the one that suits you best, and persevere in it. That is your Ishta, your special ideal.

This is the theory of the Ishta. It is the only way to make religion practically meet the necessities of different constitutions, to avoid quarreling with others, and to make real progress in spiritual life. We will be fools indeed if we give up the love of God over someone else's ideas about Him. Instead, be strong, and stand up and seek the God of Love in the way that you love best. That is the highest strength.

Jesus, the Great Prophet of Nazareth

THERE HAVE ALWAYS BEEN some giant waves in the ocean of the world. They are the signposts, here and there, directing the march of humanity. They are verily giants; their shadows covering the earth, they stand eternal. The light of God is everywhere, omnipresent; but we see it most vividly in one of the giant lamps of the earth — the Prophets, the Incarnations, the embodiments of God.

Take one of these great Messengers of Light, and compare his character with the highest ideal of God that you ever formed, and you will find that you cannot even imagine a higher ideal of God than what he actually embodies, practically realizes, and sets before us as an example. Is it wrong, therefore, to worship these embodiments as God? If they are really, actually, as high as our highest conceptions of God, what harm is there in worshiping them? Not only is there no harm, but it is a positive way of worship. These Incarnations of God have been worshiped in all ages and in all countries.

We are now going to study a little of the life of Christ, the Incarnation of the Jews. When Christ was born, the Jews were in that state which I call a state of fall between two waves; a state of conservatism, where the human mind, as it were, is tired of moving forward for the time being, and is only taking care of what it has already achieved; a state where the attention is more focused upon rituals and details than upon the great and vital problems of life.

Hemmed in by external enemies, driven back upon its own center by Roman might and Hellenic tendencies of intellect — hemmed in physically, mentally, and morally — there stood the Jewish people, with a tremendous inherent and conservative strength, which their descendants have not lost even today. They were forced to concentrate and focus all of their energies upon Jerusalem and Judaism; and, like all power when once gathered, it could not remain collected; it had to expand and expend itself. There is no power on earth that can be kept long confined within too narrow a limit. No power can be kept compressed very long without its expanding at a subsequent period.

It was the concentrated energy of the Jewish people that found expression in the rise of Christianity. The small streams formed into rivers. Gradually all the rivers joined together and became one vast, surging river. On the top of one of its mighty waves we see standing Jesus of Nazareth. In him was embodied all that was the best and greatest in his own people, the meaning for which they had struggled for ages — and he himself was the impetus for the future, not only for his own people, but also for unnumbered other peoples of the world.

Bear in mind that my view of the great Prophet of Nazareth is necessarily from the standpoint of the Orient. Many times you forget that the Nazarene was an Oriental. Notwithstanding all your attempts to paint him with blue eyes and yellow hair, the Nazarene is still Oriental. All the similes, all the imagery with which the Bible is filled — the scenes, the locations, the attitudes, the groups, the poetry and symbolism — speak of the Orient: of the bright sky, of the heat, of the sun, of the desert; of thirsty people and animals; of women coming with pitchers on their heads to fill them at the wells; of the flocks, of the farmers, of the cultivation going on all around; of the water-mill and the wheel of the mill-pond, of the millstones. All these are to be seen today in Asia.

So we find that Jesus of Nazareth was a true son of the Orient. As such, he had no faith in this evanescent world and its various belongings. He had no family ties, and no interest in property, power, or wealth. Do you think that this man had any physical ideas in him? He was the Soul — nothing but the Soul, just working through a body for the good of humanity; and that was all his relation to the body.

He had no other idea of himself, no other except that he was Spirit. He was disembodied, unfettered, unbound Spirit. And not only so, but he, with his marvelous vision, had found that every man and woman, whether Jew or Gentile, whether rich or poor, whether saint or sinner, was the embodiment of the same undying Spirit as himself. Therefore, the one work of his whole life was calling upon them to realize their own spiritual nature. Give up, he says, these superstitious dreams that you are low and that you are poor. Give up the idea that you are slaves, trampled upon and tyrannized over. Within you is something that can never be tyrannized over, never be trampled upon, never be troubled, never be killed. You are all Children of God, Eternal Spirit. "Know ye," he declared, "the kingdom of heaven is within you." Dare not only to stand up and say, "I am a Child of God," but also to find in your heart of hearts, "I and my Father are one." That was what Jesus of Nazareth said. He never talks of this world and of this life. He has nothing to do with it, except that he wants to get hold of the world as it is, give it a push, and drive it forward and onward until the whole world has reached to the effulgent Light of God, until everyone has realized his or her spiritual nature.

And so there is only one way that I, as an Oriental, wish to worship Jesus of Nazareth; that is to worship him as God. Do you mean to say that I have no right to worship him in that way? If we bring him down to our own level and simply pay him a little respect as a great man, why should we worship at all? Our scriptures say, "These great children of Light, who manifest the Light themselves, who are Light themselves, they, being worshiped, become one with us, and we become one with them."

The Prophets of India

TRUE RELIGION IS NEITHER talk, nor theory, nor intellectual consent. It is realization in our heart of hearts; it is touching God; it is feeling, realizing that I am Spirit related to the Universal Spirit and all Its great manifestations. Wherever there has been actual religion — this touch of the Divine, the soul coming in direct contact with the Divine — there has always been a broadening of the mind, which has enabled it to see the Light everywhere. We see that wherever there has been real love of God, the soul has grown Godward and has gotten a glimpse of, or has even attained to, direct perception. And when that direct perception is attained, then "all doubts vanish forever, all the crookedness of the heart is made straight, and all bondage vanishes," for God is then seen, He is then experienced, He is then realized. That is religion; that is all of religion. The rest is mere theory and dogma.

These Messengers and Prophets of God were great and true. Why so? Because each one came to preach great ideas. Take the Prophets of India. They are the oldest of the founders of religion. We take, first, Krishna. You who have read the Bhagavad Gita know that the one idea that Krishna teaches all through the book is non-attachment, remaining unattached to the evanescent things of life. The heart's love is due to only One. To whom? To Him who never changes; to God. We must love God, and only in and through Him everyone that lives. This is the keynote. You must love your wife, but not for your wife's sake, but for the sake of the Lord within her. "Never, O Beloved, is the wife loved on account of the wife, but for the sake of the Lord that is in the wife." "Never, O Beloved, is the husband loved on account of the husband, but for the sake of the Lord that is in the husband." The

Vedanta philosophy says that even in the love of husband and wife, the real attraction is the Lord, who is present there. He is the only attraction; there is no other. When we love knowing this, it is salvation, it is joy, it is freedom. When we love without knowing this, it will bring pain. So wherever there is love, wherever there is even a spark of joy, know that to be His presence, because He is joy, blessedness, and love itself. Without Him, there cannot be any love, for he *is* love.

Now, what is another message of Krishna? "Whosoever lives in the midst of the world, and works, offering all the fruit of his action unto the Lord, he is never touched by the evils of the world. Just as the lotus, born under the water, rises up and blossoms above the water, even so is the man who is engaged selflessly in the activities of the world, offering all the fruit of his activities unto the Lord." The result of this teaching is that all of the duties of the world are sanctified. There is no duty in this world that we have any right to call menial; each person's work done in this spirit is quite as good as that of an emperor on his throne.

And then there is Buddha's message — a tremendous message. Says Buddha, Root out selfishness and everything that makes you selfish. Become perfectly unselfish. As soon as selfish desires arise, as soon as some selfish pursuit is followed, immediately the whole man, the real man, is gone: he becomes like a brute, he becomes a slave to his desires, he forgets his fellow men. No more does he say, "You first and me afterward," but, "Me first, and let everyone else look out for themselves." That is why there is misery in our lives; because we are selfish.

What is the way out? Destroy the selfishness within us. Only then will we be truly happy and make others happy. Work not to get any reward, not for any superstition, but because you are seeking your own release by killing the selfishness that has you bound.

Buddha was the pinnacle of purity. Bereft of all selfishness, he did not care to go to heaven, and he did not want money. He gave up his throne and everything else, and went about the streets of India, preaching for the good of all humanity with a heart as wide as the ocean. He stands as the perfection of the active type, perfectly selfless, and the very heights to which he attained shows that through the power of work, the power of Karma Yoga, we can attain to the highest spirituality.

Will other Prophets come? Certainly they will. But do not look forward to that. Better that each one of you become a Prophet. Take all the ancient wisdom, supplement it with your own realizations, and become a Prophet unto others through your example. Each one of the Prophets has been great; each has left something for us. They have been our gods. We salute them; we are their servants. And at the same time, we salute ourselves; for if they have been Prophets and children of God, we are also the same. They reached their perfection, and we are going to attain ours. Remember the words of Jesus: "The kingdom of heaven is at hand." This very moment, let every one of us make a staunch resolution: "I will become a Prophet, I will become a messenger of Light, I will become a child of God."

The Renunciation of the Bhakta

WE HAVE NOW FINISHED the consideration of what may be called the preparatory Bhakti, and are entering into the study of Para-Bhakti, or supreme devotion. We have to speak of a preparation to the practice of this Para-Bhakti. All such preparations are intended only for the purification of the soul. The repetition of sacred names, the rituals, the forms, and the symbols, all these various things are for the purification of the soul. The greatest purifier among all such things, a purifier without which no one can enter the regions of this higher devotion, is renunciation. This frightens many; yet without it, there cannot be any spiritual growth. In all our Yogas this renunciation is necessary. It is the stepping-stone and the real center and heart of all spiritual growth.

When the human soul draws back from the illusory things of the world and tries to go deeper; when we, the Spirit which here has somehow become bound and materialized, start to understand our bondage and turn our face away from those selfish desires that bind us, then begins renunciation, then begins real spiritual growth.

Of all renunciations, the most natural is that of the Bhakti Yogi. Here there is no violence, nothing to give up or tear off from ourselves, nothing from which we have to violently separate ourselves. The Bhakta's renunciation is easy, smooth flowing, and as natural as the things around us. We see the manifestation of this sort of renunciation, more or less, every day around us. An uncultured man loves the pleasures of the senses intensely; as he becomes cultured, he begins to love intellectual pleasures, and his sense-enjoyments become less and less important to him. At first, pleasure is in association with the lowest senses; but as soon as he reaches a higher plane of existence, the lower kind of pleasures become less intense. In human society, the nearer the person is to the animal, the stronger is his pleasure in the senses; and the higher and the more cultured the person, the greater is his pleasure in intellectual and such other finer pursuits. So when a man gets even higher than the plane of the intellect, when he gets to the plane of spirituality and of divine inspiration, he finds there a state of bliss, compared with which all the pleasures of the senses, or even of the intellect, are as nothing. When the moon shines brightly, all the stars become dim; and when the sun shines, the moon itself becomes dim. The renunciation necessary for the attainment of Bhakti is not obtained by destroying anything, but it comes naturally, in the same way that in the presence of an increasingly stronger light, the less intense lights become dimmer and dimmer until they vanish away completely. So this love of the pleasures of the senses and of the intellect is all made dim and thrown aside and cast into the shade by the love of God Himself.

That love of God grows and assumes a form that is called Para-Bhakti, or supreme devotion. Forms vanish, rituals fly away, books are superseded. Images, temples, churches, religions, sects, countries, and nationalities — all these little limitations and bondages fall off by their own nature from those who know this love of God. Nothing remains to bind them or fetter their freedom. Divine grace loosens the binding bolts and bars of their souls, and they become free. So in this renunciation in favor of devotion, there is no harshness, no dryness, no struggle, no repression, and no suppression. The Bhakta has not to suppress any single one of his emotions; he only strives to intensify them and direct them to God.

Supreme Bhakti, Supreme Devotion

NOW WE COME TO what is called supreme Bhakti, supreme devotion, when the forms and symbols of preparatory Bhakti have fallen off. Those who have reached supreme Bhakti cannot belong to any one religion, for all religions are in them. To what shall they belong? Where is there a church big enough for them? Such people cannot bind themselves down to certain limited forms. Where is the limit for unlimited love, with which they have become one? The joy of even human love is but a faint echo of the blissful love of these saints for God. The true lovers of God become what Emerson calls "God-intoxicated." They drink of the cup of love, which has been prepared by the saints of every religion, who have poured their hearts' blood into it, and in which has been concentrated all the hopes of those who wanted to love God for love's sake only, without seeking reward. The reward of love is love, and what a reward it is! It is the only thing that takes off all sorrows, the only cup by the drinking of which the illusory sufferings of the world vanish.

All the various systems of religion, in the end, converge to that one point, that perfect union. We always begin as dualists. God is a separate being and I am a separate being. Love comes between, and a man begins to approach God, and God, as it were, begins to approach the man. Man takes up all the various relationships of life; and the last point is reached when he becomes one with the object of his worship. "I am you, and you are me, and in worshiping you, I worship myself, and in worshiping myself, I worship you." There we find the highest culmination of that with which man begins. That God who at first was a Being somewhere, became resolved, as it were, into Infinite Love. Man himself was also transformed. He was approaching God, and, in doing so, was throwing off all vain desires with which he was full before. As these vain desires vanished, so did all selfishness, and, at the apex, he found that Love, Lover, and Beloved were One.

Raja Yoga

Oneness through Mastery of Mind

SWAMI VIVEKANANDA, LONDON, 1896

Introduction to Raja Yoga

RELIGION, AS IT IS generally taught all over the world, is found to be based upon faith and belief, and in most cases consists only of different sets of theories; and that is why we find religions quarreling with one another. Nevertheless, there is a basis of universal belief in religion that governs all the different theories and all the varying ideas of different sects in different countries. Going to this basis, we find that they are based upon universal *experiences.*

If you go to the fountainhead of Christianity, you will find that it is based upon experience. Christ said that he saw God, the disciples said that they felt God, and so on. Similarly, in Buddhism, it was Buddha's experience that was taught. He experienced certain truths, saw them, came in contact with them, and preached them to the world. So with the Hindus. In their books, the writers, called *rishis,* or sages, declare that they have experienced certain truths, and these they preach.

Thus it is clear that all the religions of the world have been built upon that one universal and unshakable foundation of all our knowledge — direct experience. The teachers all saw God; they all saw their own souls, they saw their soul's future and their eternity; and what these teachers saw they preached. But since then there has been this difference: Most of these religions, especially in modern times, claim that these experiences are impossible to others; that they were possible only to a few men who were the founders of the religions that subsequently bore their names. They say that these experiences are not available to us, and therefore, we now have to take these religions on faith.

This is completely false. If there has been one experience in this world in any particular branch of knowledge, it absolutely follows that that experience has been possible countless times before and will be repeated countless times in the future. Uniformity is the rigorous law of nature: what happened once can happen again and again.

The teachers of the science of Yoga declare not only that religion is based upon the experiences of ancient times, but also that no man can be religious until he has had the same experiences himself. Yoga is the science that teaches us how to attain these experiences ourselves. It is not much use to talk about religion until one has felt it.

There has been more bloodshed in the name of God than for any other cause, because people never went to the fountainhead; they were content to give only a mental assent to the customs of their forefathers, and wanted others to do the same. What right has a man to say that he has a soul if he does not feel it, or that there is a God if he does not see Him? If there is a God, we must see Him; if there is a soul, we must perceive it. Otherwise, it is better not to believe. It is better to be an outspoken atheist than a hypocrite.

People want truth; they want to experience truth for themselves. When they have grasped it, realized it, felt it within their hearts, then alone, declare the Vedas, will all doubts vanish, all darkness be scattered, and all crookedness be made straight. "Ye children of immortality, the way is found. There is a way out of this darkness, and that is by perceiving Him who is beyond all darkness. There is no other way."

The science of Raja Yoga proposes to put before humanity a practical and scientifically worked out method of reaching this truth. In the first place, every science must have its own method of investigation. If you want to become an astronomer, and you sit down and cry, "Astronomy! Astronomy!" you will never become one. It is the same with chemistry. A certain method must be followed. You must go to a laboratory, take different substances, mix them, compound them, and experiment with them; out of that will come a knowledge of chemistry. If you want to be an astronomer, you must go to an observatory, take a telescope, and study the stars and planets. And then you will become an astronomer.

Each science has its own methods. I could preach you thousands of sermons, but they would not make you religious until you followed the method. This truth has been preached by sages of all countries and of all ages, by people pure and unselfish, who had no motive but to do good to the world. They all declare that they have found certain truths higher than what the senses can bring us, and they invite verification. They ask us to take up the discipline and practice honestly. Then, if we do not find this higher truth, we shall have the right to say that there is no truth in the claim; but before we have done that, we are not rational in denying the truth of their assertions. So we must work faithfully, using the prescribed methods, and light will come.

In acquiring knowledge, we make use of generalization based upon observation. We must first observe facts, then generalize, and then draw conclusions or formulate principles. The knowledge of the mind, of thought, of the internal nature of the human being, can never be had until we have first developed the power of observing what is going on within. It is comparatively easy to observe facts in the external world, for many instruments have been invented for such a purpose; but in the internal world, we have no instrument to help us. Yet we know that we must observe in order to have a real science. Without proper analysis, any science will be mere theorizing; and that is why the psychologists have been quarreling among themselves since the beginning of time, except those few who found out the means of observation.

The science of Raja Yoga proposes to give us such a means of observing the internal states. The instrument is the mind itself. The power of attention, when properly guided and directed toward the internal world, will analyze the mind and illumine facts for us. The powers of the mind are like rays of light dissipated; when they are concentrated, they illumine.

From childhood onward we have been taught to pay attention only to things external, but never to things internal; hence most of us have nearly lost the faculty of observing the internal mechanism. To turn the mind, as it were, inside; to stop it from going outside, and then to concentrate all of its powers and throw them upon itself, so that it may know and analyze its own nature, is very hard work. Yet that is the only way to anything which will be like a scientific approach to the subject.

In Raja Yoga, the powers of the mind are to be concentrated and turned back upon the mind; and as the darkest places reveal their secrets before the penetrating rays of the sun, so will the concentrated mind penetrate into its own innermost secrets. Thus will we come to genuine religion. Then we shall perceive for ourselves whether or not we have souls, whether or not life lasts for five minutes or for eternity, whether or not there is a God. All this will be revealed to us. This is what Raja Yoga proposes to teach. And in its study, no faith or belief is necessary. Believe nothing until you find it out for yourself — that is what it teaches us. Truth requires no prop to make it stand.

Raja: The Yoga of Concentration

THE FIRST TEST OF true teaching must be that the teaching should not contradict reason. And you will see that such is the basis of all these Yogas. Now first of all, let me take up Raja Yoga, the psychological Yoga, the psychological way to union. It is a vast subject, and I can only point out to you now the central idea of this Yoga. We have but one method of acquiring knowledge. From the lowest man to the highest Yogi, all have to use the same method; and that method is what is called concentration. The chemist who works in his laboratory concentrates all the powers of his mind, brings them into one focus, and throws them on the elements; and the elements stand analyzed, and thus his knowledge comes. The astronomer concentrates the powers of his mind and brings them into one focus; and he throws them onto objects through his telescope; and stars and systems roll forward and give up their secrets to him. So it is in every case with every person who is working to know. You are hearing me, and if my words interest you, your mind will become concentrated on them; and even if a clock strikes, you will not hear it on account of this concentration. The more you are able to concentrate your mind, the better you will understand me; and the more I concentrate my love and powers, the better I shall be able to give expression to what I want to convey to you. The more this power of concentration, the more knowledge is acquired, because this is the one and only method of acquiring knowledge. Even the most menial laborer, if he gives more concentration, will work better.

In making money, or in worshiping God, or in doing anything, the stronger the power of concentration, the better will that thing be done. This is the one call, the one knock that opens the gates of nature and lets out floods of light. This, the power of concentration, is the only key to the treasure-house of knowledge. The system of Raja Yoga deals almost exclusively with this. In our present state, we are so distracted that the mind is constantly frittering away its energies upon all sorts of vain and trivial things. How to concentrate the mind, how to bring the mind completely under our control, is the whole subject of study in Raja Yoga.

The Liberation of the Soul

SINCE THE DAWN OF history, various extraordinary mental phenomena have been recorded as happening among human beings. In India, such phenomena have been studied, investigated, and generalized for thousands of years. The whole ground of the religious faculties of man has been analyzed; and the practical result is the science of Raja Yoga.

Raja Yoga does not deny the existence of facts that are difficult to explain; on the contrary, it gently, and yet in no uncertain terms, tells the superstitious that miracles and answers to prayer and powers of faith, though true as facts, are not rendered comprehensible through superstitious explanations attributing them to the agency of a being or beings above the clouds. It declares the truth that each of us is a conduit for the infinite ocean of knowledge and power that lies behind humankind. It teaches that desires and wants are in us, along with the power of supply, and that wherever and whenever a desire, a want, or a prayer has been fulfilled, it was out of this infinite magazine that the fulfillment came, and not from any supernatural being. The idea of supernatural beings may rouse to a certain extent the power of action in us, but it also brings spiritual decay. It brings dependence; it brings fear; it brings superstition. It degenerates into a horrible belief in the natural weakness of man. All the orthodox systems of Indian philosophy have one goal in view: the liberation of the soul through perfection. The method is Yoga.

Each soul is potentially divine, and the goal of Yoga is to manifest this Divinity within by controlling nature, external and internal. We can do this either by work (Karma Yoga) or worship (Bhakti Yoga) or psychic control (Raja Yoga) or knowledge (Jnana

Yoga) — by one or more or all of these, and when we do, we shall be free. Always remember that the bringing forth of the Divinity within us is the whole of religion. Doctrines, dogmas, rituals, and books are but secondary details.

Raja: The Yoga of Psychology

PSYCHOLOGY IS THE SCIENCE of sciences; but in the West it is put on the same plane as the other sciences; that is, it is judged by the same criterion — utility. How much will it add to our growing happiness? How much will it detract from our increasing pain? Such, it seems, is the criterion by which everything is judged in the West.

People seem to forget that about 90 percent of all our knowledge cannot be applied in any practical way to add to our material happiness or to lessen our misery. Only the smallest fraction of our scientific knowledge can have any such practical application to our daily life. This is so because only an infinitely small percentage of our conscious mind is on the sense plane. We live in just a little bit of sense-consciousness, and we imagine that to be our entire mind and life; but as a matter of fact, it is but a drop in the mighty ocean of the subconscious mind.

If all there is of us were a bundle of sense-perceptions, then all the knowledge we could gain could be utilized in the gratification of our sense-pleasures. But fortunately, such is not the case. As we get further and further away from the animal state, our sense-pleasures become less and less important, and our enjoyment, in a rapidly increasing consciousness of scientific and psychological knowledge, becomes more and more intense. And then "knowledge for the sake of knowledge," regardless of the amount of sense-pleasures it may or may not lead to, becomes the supreme pleasure of the mind.

But even taking the Western idea of utility as the criterion by which to judge psychology, it is still the science of sciences. Why? Because we are all slaves to our senses, slaves to our own minds, conscious and subconscious. The reason why a criminal is a criminal is not because he desires to be one, but because he does not have his mind under control, and is therefore a slave to his conscious and subconscious mind. He must follow the dominant trend of his mind; he cannot help it. He is forced onward in spite of himself, in spite of his own better instincts and his own better nature; he is forced to obey the dominant mandate of his own mind.

We see this in our own lives constantly. We are constantly doing things against the better side of our nature, and afterward we scold ourselves for doing so and wonder what we could have been thinking of, how we could have done such a thing! Yet again and again we do it, and again and again we suffer for it and criticize ourselves. At the time, perhaps, we think we desire to do it, but we only desire it because we are forced to desire it. We are forced onward by the promptings of our minds, and until we realize it, we are helpless to change it. We are slaves to our minds; whether we are good or bad, that makes no difference. We are led here and there because our minds tell us to go here and there, and we cannot help ourselves because we don't see our slavery. We say we think and we say we do, but it is not so. We think because we have to think, and we act because we are forced to act.

Deep down in our subconscious minds are stored up all of the thoughts and acts of the past. The great ocean of subjective mind is full of these past thoughts and actions. Each one of them is striving to be recognized, pushing outward for expression, surging, wave after wave, out upon the objective mind, the conscious mind. These thoughts, and their stored-up energy, we take for natural desires. This is because we do not realize their true origin. We obey them blindly, unquestioningly; and slavery, the most helpless kind of slavery, is the result. Yet we call ourselves free. Free? We who cannot govern our own minds? We who cannot hold our minds on a subject, focus it on a point to the exclusion of everything else for even a moment? Think of it! Some sense-desire crops up, and immediately we obey it. Our conscience smites us for such weakness, but again and again we do it; we are always doing it.

It is the science of psychology that teaches us how to hold in check the wild gyrations and cravings of the mind, how to place it under the control of the will, and thus how to free ourselves from its tyrannical mandates. The mind uncontrolled and unguided will drag us down forever — it will tear us apart, kill us; and the mind controlled and guided will save us, free us. So it must be controlled, and psychology teaches us how to do it. The greatest science, therefore, is the science of the mind, the science of psychology. In India, that study, and its practice and perfection, is called Raja Yoga.

The Grand Science of Yoga

THE STUDY OF RAJA YOGA takes constant practice. A part of this practice is physical, but in the main it is mental. As we proceed we shall find how intimately the mind is connected with the body. When one is angry, the mind becomes disturbed; and when the mind is disturbed, the body also becomes disturbed. With the majority of humanity, the mind is greatly under the control of the body, their minds and their power of control being very little developed. People have very little command of their minds. Therefore, to bring that command about, to get that control over body and mind, we must first take certain physical steps. Then, when the body is sufficiently controlled, we can attempt to bring the mind under our control, make it work as we choose, and compel it to concentrate its powers as we desire.

According to the Raja Yogi, the external world is but the gross form of the internal, or subtle world. The external world is the effect, and the internal, the cause. Those who have discovered and learned how to control the internal forces will get the whole of nature under their control.

The end and aim of all science is to find the Unity out of which the manifold is manufactured, the One appearing as many. Raja Yoga proposes to start from the internal world, study internal nature, and through that, control the whole — both internal and external. It is a very old attempt, and India has been its special stronghold. However, for various reasons, it fell into the hands of persons who tried to make a great secret of this sacred wisdom.

Anything that is secret and mysterious in this system of Yoga should be at once rejected. The best guide in life is strength. In religion, as in all other matters, discard everything that weakens you; have nothing to do with it. Mystery-mongering weakens the human brain. It had almost destroyed Yoga, one of the grandest of sciences. From the time it was discovered, more than four thousand years ago, Yoga had been perfectly delineated, formulated, and preached in India. Then Yoga fell into the hands of persons who made it a secret, instead of letting the full blaze of daylight and reason fall upon it. They did so that they might have the powers to themselves.

There is no mystery in what I shall teach. What I know I will tell you, but you must not blindly believe. You must exercise your own reason and judgment, and learn from your own experience whether these things are true or not. Just as you would take up any other science, exactly in the same manner should you take up the study of this grand science of Yoga.

Realization Is Real Religion

The Yogis tell us that we get our knowledge of ordinary objects by direct perception, inference, or the testimony of people who are competent. By "people who are competent," the Yogis mean the Rishis, or the Seers of the thoughts recorded in the scriptures — the Vedas. According to them, the scriptures alone cannot take us to realization. We can read all the Vedas, and yet still not realize anything. But when we practice the teachings faithfully, they tell us that we can attain to that state that makes real what the scriptures proclaim is Truth, which penetrates where neither reason nor perception nor inference can go, and where the testimony of others cannot avail.

Realization is real religion; all the rest is only preparation. Hearing lectures, reading books, or reasoning is merely preparing the ground; it is not religion. Intellectual assent and intellectual dissent are also not religion. The central idea of the Yogis is that just as we come into direct contact with objects of the senses, so too can religion be directly perceived, and even in a far more intense sense. The truths of religion, such as God and Soul, cannot be perceived by the external senses. We cannot see God with our eyes, nor can we touch Him with our hands. We also cannot reason beyond the senses. Reason leaves us at a point quite indecisive; we may reason all our lives, as the world has been doing for thousands of years, and the result will still be that we are incompetent to prove or disprove the facts of religion.

What we perceive directly we take as the basis, and upon that basis we reason. So it is obvious that reasoning has to run within these bounds of perception; it cannot go beyond. The whole scope of realization, therefore, is beyond sense-perception. The Yogis say that we can go beyond our direct sense-perception, and beyond our reason also. We have within us the faculty and the power of transcending even our intellect, a power that is in every being, every creature. By the practice of Yoga that power is aroused, and when it is, then and only then can we transcend the ordinary limits of reason, and, established in Spirit, directly perceive the Infinite beyond all reason.

The Eight Steps of Raja Yoga

RAJA YOGA IS DIVIDED into eight steps. The first is *Yama*, which includes non-harmfulness, truthfulness, non-stealing, continence, and non-greed. Next is *Niyama*, consisting of cleanliness, contentment, austerity, study, and self-surrender to God. Then comes *Asana*, or posture; *Pranayama*, or control of the life force; *Pratyahara*, or restraint of the senses from their objects; *Dharana*, or fixing the mind on a spot; *Dhyana*, or meditation; and *Samadhi*, or superconscious experience. Yama and Niyama are moral training, without which no practice of yoga will succeed. As the yogi becomes established in these, he will begin to realize the fruits of his practice; without them, it will never bear fruit.

Yama, the first of the eight steps, is the practice of self-restraint and self-denial. The immense possibilities of divine realization in the soul cannot get actualized without a struggle against our lower nature. Without such struggle on the part of the aspiring devotee, no progress can be made. Purity of heart, mind, and body is absolutely the basic discipline, the bedrock upon which the building of godliness rests. Cleansing the external body and being discriminating about food are both easy, but without internal purity these external observances are of no value whatsoever. Therefore, we must always remember that external practices have value only as they help to develop internal purity.

The qualities conducive to purity are: truthfulness, sincerity, doing good to others without thought of gain for one's self; not harming others by thought, word, or deed; not coveting another's goods; not thinking vain or selfish thoughts; and not brooding over injuries received from another. In this list, the idea that deserves special notice is *Ahimsa*, non-injury to others. A yogi must strive never to cause harm to anyone by thought, word, or deed. Mercy must not be for men and women alone, but must go beyond and embrace the whole world. This duty of non-injury, even in thought, is obligatory for the aspirant in relation to all beings. The person whose heart never holds even the thought of harm to anyone is a true yogi.

Prana and Akasha

PRANAYAMA IS NOT, as many think, concerned solely with the breath; breath indeed has very little to do with it. Breathing is only one of the many exercises through which we get to the real Pranayama. Pranayama means the control of *Prana,* the manifesting power of the universe.

According to the philosophers of India, the universe is composed of two entities, one of which they call *Akasha,* and the other, Prana. Akasha is the all-penetrating existence. Everything that has form, everything that is the result of combination, is evolved out of Akasha. It is Akasha that becomes the air, that becomes the liquids, and that becomes the solids; it is Akasha that becomes the sun, the earth, the moon, the stars, and the comets; it is Akasha that becomes the human body, the animal body, the plants, every form that we see, everything that can be sensed, and everything that exists.

Akasha cannot be perceived; it is so subtle that it is beyond all ordinary perception. It can be seen only when it has become material and has taken a form. At the beginning of creation, there is only Akasha; at the end of the cycle, all solids, liquids, and gases melt into Akasha again, and the next creation similarly proceeds out of Akasha.

By what power is Akasha manufactured into this universe? By the power of Prana. Just as Akasha is the omnipresent material of this universe, so is Prana the infinite, omnipresent manifesting power of this universe. At the beginning and at the end of a cycle, all tangible objects resolve back into Akasha, and all the forces in the universe resolve back into Prana. In the next cycle, out of this

Prana is evolved everything that we call energy, everything that we call force.

It is Prana that is manifesting as motion; it is Prana that is manifesting as gravitation, as magnetism. It is Prana that is manifesting as the actions of the body, as the nerve currents, and as thought-force. From thought down to physical force, everything is but the manifestation of Prana. The sum total of all forces in the universe, mental or physical, when resolved back to their original state, is called Prana.

At the end of a cycle, the energies now displayed in the universe quiet down and become potential. At the beginning of the next cycle, they start up, strike upon Akasha, and thus out of Akasha evolve these various forms; and as Akasha changes, Prana changes also into all these manifestations of energy. The knowledge and control of Prana is really what is meant by Pranayama.

Just as this whole universe and beyond has been generalized in the Vedas into that one Absolute Existence, and those who have grasped that Existence have grasped the whole universe, so all forces have been generalized into Prana, and those who have grasped Prana have grasped all the forces of the universe. The person who has control of Prana has control of his or her own mind and body, because Prana is the source of all energy.

How to control Prana is the sole idea of Pranayama. All the trainings and exercises in this regard are for that one end. We must begin where we stand, must learn how to control the things that are nearest to us. This body is very near to us, nearer than anything in the external universe; and the mind is nearer than the body. But the Prana that is working this mind and body is the nearest. It is a part of the Prana that moves the universe. In the infinite ocean of Prana, this little wave of Prana that represents our own energies, mental and physical, is the Prana nearest to us. The yogi who learns to control his or her little wave gains perfection.

Meditations and Mantra

THE SENSE ORGANS ARE always acting outward and coming in contact with external objects. Bringing them under the control of the will is what is called Pratyahara, or gathering toward oneself. Fixing the mind on the lotus of the heart, or on the center of the head, is what is called Dharana. Limited to one spot, a particular kind of mental wave rises; they are not swallowed up by other kinds of waves, but by degrees become prominent, while all the others recede and finally disappear. Then the multiplicity of these waves gives way to unity, and one wave only is left in the mind. This is Dhyana, meditation. When the whole of the mind has become one wave, when only the meaning, the essence of the thought is present, it is called Samadhi. If the mind can be fixed on the lotus of the heart or the center of the head for twelve seconds, it will be a Dharana, twelve such Dharanas will be a Dhyana, and twelve such Dhyanas will be a Samadhi.

A few examples are given of what to meditate upon. Sit straight, and imagine a lotus upon the top of the head, several inches up, with virtue as its center, and knowledge as its stalk. Inside of that lotus think of the Golden One, the Almighty, the Intangible, He whose name is Om, the Inexpressible, surrounded with effulgent light. Meditate on that.

Another meditation is given. Think of a space in your heart, and in the midst of that space think that a flame is burning. Think of that flame as your own soul and inside the flame is another effulgent light, and that is the Soul of your soul, God. Meditate upon that in the heart.

There is a Mantra called the *Gayatri*. It is a very holy verse of the Vedas. *"We meditate on the glory of that Being who has produced this universe; may He enlighten our minds."* The word *Om* is joined to the beginning and the end of each Gayatri. Meditate on that.

Remember that non-injury, forgiveness, truth, and faith in the Lord, these are all different vows of the yogi. Be not afraid if you are not perfect in these; work, and they will come. He who has given up anger, fear, and attachment; he who has taken refuge in the Lord, whose heart has become purified, with whatsoever desire he comes to the Lord, He will grant that to him. Therefore, worship Him through knowledge, love, service, or renunciation.

"He who hates none, who is the friend of all, who is merciful to all, who is free from egoism and selfishness, who is even-minded in pain and pleasure, who is patient, who does not take offense, who works always in Yoga, whose self has become controlled, whose will is firm, whose mind and intellect are given up unto Me, such a one is My beloved. He from whom comes no disturbance, who cannot be disturbed by others, who is pure and active, and who feels blessed with what comes his way, such a one is My beloved."

Pratyahara

THE PERSON WHO HAS succeeded in attaching or detaching his mind to or from the senses at will has succeeded in *Pratyahara,* which means "gathering toward," checking the outgoing powers of the mind, freeing it from the thraldom of the senses. When we can do this, we shall really possess character; then alone shall we have taken a long step toward freedom. Before that, we are mere machines.

How hard it is to control the mind! Well has it been compared to the maddened monkey. There was a monkey, restless by his own nature, as all monkeys are. As if that were not enough, someone made him drink freely of wine, so that he became still more restless. Then a scorpion stung him, and the poor monkey found his condition worse than ever. To complete his misery, a demon entered into him. What can describe the uncontrollable restlessness of a monkey in this condition? The human mind! The human mind is like that monkey, incessantly active by its own nature; then it becomes drunk with the wine of selfish desire, thus increasing its turbulence. After desire takes possession comes the sting of the scorpion of jealousy at the success of others. And last of all, the demon of pride enters the mind, making it think of itself as so important. How hard to control such a mind!

The first lesson in Pratyahara, then, is to sit for some time and let the mind run on. The mind is bubbling up all the time. It is like that monkey jumping about. Let the monkey jump as much as he can; you simply wait and watch. Knowledge is power, says the proverb, and that is true. Until you know what the mind is doing, you cannot control it. Give it the rein; many hideous thoughts may come into it. You will be astonished that it was possible for you to think such thoughts. But you will find that each day the mind's churnings are becoming less and less violent, that each day it is becoming calmer. In the first few months, you will find that the mind will have a great many thoughts. Later, you will find that they have somewhat decreased, and in a few more months, they will be fewer and fewer, until at last the mind will be under perfect control; but you must patiently practice every day.

This controlling of the mind, and not allowing it to join itself to the sense centers, is Pratyahara. How is this practiced? It is a tremendous work, not to be done in a day. Only after a patient, continuous struggle for years will you succeed.

The End and Aim of Yoga Is Realizing God

CONCENTRATION IS THE ESSENCE of all knowledge; nothing can be done without it. Ninety percent of thought force is wasted by the ordinary human being, and therefore he is constantly committing blunders; the trained person or mind almost never makes mistakes. When the mind is concentrated and turned backward on itself, all powers within us will be our servants, and no longer our masters. The Greeks applied their concentration to the external world, and the result was perfection in art, literature, and so on. The Hindu concentrated on the internal world, upon the unseen realms in the Self, and developed the science of Yoga. Raja Yoga is the science of controlling the senses, will, and mind. The benefit of its study is that we learn to control, instead of being controlled.

Mind is layer on layer. Our real goal is to cross all these intervening strata of our being and find God. The end and aim of Yoga is to realize God. To do this, we must go beyond relative knowledge, go beyond the sense world. There is only one way to gain mastery over the senses, and that is to see Him, who is the Reality in the universe, everywhere. Then and only then will we conquer our senses.

Restraining the Mind

THE WAVES OF THOUGHT in the mind are called *vrittis* in Sanskrit, literally meaning "whirlpools." Thought is a force, as is gravitation or repulsion. From the infinite storehouse of force in nature, the instrument called mind takes hold of some, absorbs it, and sends it out as thought. Force is supplied to us through food, and out of that food the body obtains the power of motion, etc. Others, the finer forces, it throws out in what we call thought. The mind is not intelligent; yet it appears to be intelligent. Why? Because the intelligent soul is behind it. You are the only sentient being; the mind is only the instrument through which you catch the external world.

The real person is behind the mind; the mind is the instrument in his hands. It is his intelligence that is percolating through the mind. It is only when you stand behind the mind that it becomes intelligent. When a man gives up his body, his mind falls to pieces and is nothing. Thus you understand what is meant by mind. The vrittis are the waves and ripples rising in the mind when external causes impinge on it. We live in these waves of thought; they are our universe.

The bottom of a lake we cannot see, because its surface is covered with ripples. It is possible for us to catch a glimpse of the bottom only when the ripples have subsided, and the water is calm. If the water is muddy or is agitated all the time, the bottom will not be seen. If it is clear, and there are no waves, we shall see the bottom. The bottom of the lake is our Spirit, our true Self; the lake is the mind, and the waves are the vrittis.

There is the state called *sattva*, serenity, calmness, in which the waves cease, and the water of the mind-lake becomes clear. It is not an inactive state, but rather an intensely active one. In its calmness is found the greatest manifestation of power.

It is easy to be active. Let the reins go and the horses will run anywhere they wish. Anyone can do that. But the person who can stop the plunging horses is the strong one. Which requires the greater strength: letting go or restraining? You must not mistake this sattva for dullness or laziness. The calm person is the one who alone has great control over the mind waves, and his or her calmness is the manifestation of superior strength.

The mind is always trying to get back to its natural and pure state, but the senses draw it out. To restrain it, to check its outward tendency, and to start it on the return journey to the Essence of Intelligence, is the first step in Raja Yoga, because only in this way can the mind get on its proper course.

The Samskaras

THERE IS A CLASS OF thought waves called *vikalpa*. A word is uttered and we do not wait to consider its meaning; we jump to a conclusion immediately. It is the sign of weakness of the mind. Now you can understand the theory of restraint. The weaker the person, the less he or she has of this restraint. Examine yourself always by that test. When you are going to be angry or miserable, reason it out how it is that some news that has come to you is throwing your mind into one of these negative states.

These thought waves can only be controlled by practice and non-attachment. The mind, in order to have non-attachment, must be clear, good, and rational. Why should we practice? Because each thought wave is like the pulsations quivering over the surface of a lake. The vibration dies out, and what is left? The *samskaras*, the impressions. When a large number of these impressions are left on the mind, they coalesce and become a habit. It is said, "Habit is second nature," but it is first nature also; everything that we have become is the result of habit. That gives us consolation, because if it is only habit, we can make and unmake it at any time. The samskaras are left by these vibrations passing out of our mind, with each one of them leaving its result. Our character is the sum total of these marks, and accordingly, as some particular wave prevails, we take on its tone. If good prevails, one becomes good; if wickedness prevails, one becomes wicked; and if joyfulness prevails, one becomes happy. The only remedy for bad habits is counter-habits; all the bad habits that have left their impressions are to be controlled by good habits. Go on doing good and thinking holy thoughts continuously; that is the only way to subdue base impressions. Never say that any person is hopeless, because each person represents only a character, a bundle of habits that can be checked by new and better ones. Character is repeated habits, and repeated habits alone can reform character.

Continuous struggle to keep thought waves perfectly restrained is practice. Practice is the attempt to restrain the mind, to prevent its going out into waves. The mind becomes firmly grounded by long and constant efforts made with great love. Restraint does not come in one day, but only through continued practice.

Subduing the Mind Waves

YOU REMEMBER THAT OUR goal is to perceive the Soul itself. We cannot yet perceive the Soul, because it has gotten mingled up with nature, with the mind, and with the body. The ignorant person thinks that his body is the Soul. The learned person thinks that his mind is the Soul. But both of them are mistaken. What makes the Soul get mingled up with all this? Different waves in the mind rise and cover the Soul, and we can only see a little reflection of the Soul through these waves. So if the wave is one of anger, we see the Soul as angry; "I am angry," we say. If it is one of love, we see ourselves reflected in that wave, and we say that we are loving. And if the wave is one of weakness, we see the Soul as weak, and we say, "I am weak." These various ideas come from these impressions, these samskaras, covering the Soul. The real nature of the Soul is not perceived as long as there is a single wave in the lake of the mind; this real nature will not be perceived until all the waves have subsided. So first, Patanjali teaches us the meaning of these waves; second, he teaches us the best way to subdue them; and third, he teaches us how to make one wave so strong as to suppress all other waves, fire eating fire, as it were. When only one remains, it will be easy to suppress that also, and when that is gone, this Samadhi, or concentration, leaves nothing, and the Soul is manifested just as It is, in Its own glory. Then alone will we know that the Soul is not a compound; It is the One Eternal Substance in the universe, and as such, It cannot be born and It cannot die. It is immortal, indestructible, the ever-living Essence of Intelligence.

Dharana and Samyama

DHARANA, CONCENTRATION, IS WHEN the mind holds onto some particular object, either in the body or outside the body, and keeps itself in that state. An unbroken flow of knowledge in that object is Dhyana, meditation. The mind tries to think of one object, to hold itself to one particular spot, such as the heart or the top of the head, and if the mind succeeds in receiving the sensations only through that part of the body, and through no other part, that would be Dharana. When the mind succeeds in keeping itself in that state for some time, it is called Dhyana. When this meditation reflects only the meaning, the essence of the object being meditated on, it is Samadhi. This comes when in meditation the form, or the external part, is completely given up. When I succeed in concentrating the mind to the point of perceiving only the essence of the object, unexpressed in any form — that state of Dhyana is called Samadhi.

These three, Dharana, Dhyana, and Samadhi, when practiced together in regard to one object, is called *Samyama*. When we can direct our mind to any particular object and fix it there, and then keep it there for a long time, separating the object from the internal part, this is Samyama; Dharana, Dhyana, and Samadhi, one following the other, and made one. The form of the thing has vanished, and only its meaning remains in the mind.

When a person has succeeded in making this Samyama, all powers come under his or her control. By making Samyama on friendship, mercy, or other blessed qualities, the Yogi will come to excel in those respective qualitites. By the conquest of Samyama comes the light of knowledge. This is the great instrument of the Yogi.

Dhyana and Samadhi

IN ORDER TO REACH the superconscious state in a scientific manner, it is necessary to pass through the various steps of Raja Yoga. After Pratyahara and Dharana, we come to Dhyana, meditation. When the mind has been trained to remain fixed on a certain internal or external location, there comes to it the power of flowing in an unbroken current toward that point. This state is called Dhyana. When one has so intensified the power of Dhyana as to be able to reject the external part of perception and remain meditating only on the internal part, the meaning, the essence, that state is called Samadhi. The three — Dharana, Dhyana, and Samadhi — together are called Samyama. That is, if the mind can first concentrate upon an object, and then is able to continue in that concentration for a length of time, and then, by continued concentration, is able to dwell only on the internal part of the perception of which the object was the effect, everything comes under the control of such a mind.

This meditative state is the highest state of existence. It is only the contemplative, witness-like study of objects that brings to us real enjoyment and happiness. So long as there is sense desire, no real happiness can come. The animal has its happiness in the senses, the man in his intellect, and the God-man in spiritual contemplation. It is only to the soul that has attained to this contemplative state that the world really becomes beautiful. To those who live beyond the desires of the senses and do not mix themselves up with them, the manifold changes of nature are one panorama of beauty and sublimity.

In true spiritual contemplation, a Yogi will be able to see the very foundations of his mind, and it will be under his perfect control. As a result, he will attain to the goal of Raja Yoga, the complete suppression of the waves in the ocean of the mind. Then, the glory of the soul, undisturbed by the distractions of the mind or the motions of the body, will shine in its full effulgence; and the Yogi will find himself as he is and as he always was, the Essence of Knowledge, the Immortal, the All-Pervading and Eternal Spirit.

Meditation

THE MEDITATIVE STATE OF mind is declared by the Yogis to be the highest state in which the mind exists. When the mind is studying the external object, it gets identified with it and loses itself. To use the simile of the old Indian philosopher, the human soul is like a piece of crystal, in that it takes the color of whatever is near it. Whatever the soul touches, it takes its color, and that is the difficulty. That is what constitutes the bondage. The color is so strong, the crystal forgets itself and identifies itself with the color. Suppose a red flower is near the crystal, and the crystal takes the color and forgets itself, thinking it is red. In the same way, we have taken the color of our *body*, and as a result, we have forgotten what we truly are. All the difficulties that follow come from our identification with the body. All of our fears, worries, anxieties, troubles, mistakes, weaknesses, and evils are from this one great blunder — believing that we are our bodies. This is the lot of the ordinary person, even though we are no more our bodies than the crystal is the red flower.

It is through the practice of meditation that the crystal discovers what it truly is, that it realizes its own color. It is meditation that brings us nearer to Truth than anything else.

In India, two persons meet. In English they say, "How do you do?" But the Indian greeting is, "Are you upon yourself?" The moment you stand upon something else, you run the risk of being miserable. This is what I mean by meditation — the soul trying to stand upon itself. That state must surely be the healthiest state of the soul, when it is thinking of itself, the Eternal Spirit, and residing in its own glory.

There are three stages in meditation. The first is what is called Dharana, or concentration. It is the concentrating of the mind upon an object. I try to concentrate my mind upon this glass, excluding every other object from my mind except this glass. But the mind wavers. When it has become strong and does not waver so much, it is called Dhyana, or meditation. And then there is a still higher state when the differentiation between the glass and myself is lost, and this is called Samadhi, or absorption. The mind and the glass become one.

If you want power over nature, you can have it through meditation. It is through the power of meditation that all scientific facts are discovered today. Scientists study the subject before them and forget everything — forget their own identity and everything else — and then the great discoveries come like a flash. Therein you see the power of meditation — intensity of thought. These men and women churn up their own souls. As a result, great truths come to the surface and become manifest. Therefore, the practice of meditation is the great scientific method of knowledge. There is no knowledge without the power of meditation.

You are the Spirit. That is the first fundamental belief you must never give up. You are the Spirit within you. All of this skill of Yoga and this system of meditation is just to find Him there. Why am I saying all this now? Because until you fix the location, you cannot talk. We have fixed the location up in heaven and all the world over except in the right place. I am Spirit, and therefore the Spirit of all spirits must be in my soul. Those who think it somewhere else don't yet understand the truth. It is to be sought and found here, in this heaven within. There are sages who, knowing this, turn their eyes inward and find the Spirit of all spirits in their own souls. That is the scope and the aim of meditation. Find out for yourself the truth about God and about your own soul, for when you do, you shall be free.

The Ocean of Perfection

THE WATER FOR IRRIGATION of fields is already in the canal, only shut in by gates. The farmer opens these gates, and the water flows in by itself, by the law of gravitation. So all progress and power are already in every person; perfection is our nature, only it is barred in and prevented from taking its proper course. If anyone can take the bar off, in rushes nature. Then we attain the powers that are already ours. Those we once called wicked become saints as soon as the bar is lifted and nature rushes in. It is nature that is driving us toward perfection, and eventually she will bring everyone there. All these practices and struggles to become religious are only the work of ridding ourselves of the obstacles, of taking off the bars, of opening the doors to that perfection that is our birthright, our nature.

Patanjali, the great ancient evolutionist, declared that the secret and true meaning of evolution is the manifestation of the perfection that is already in every being; that this perfection has been barred and the infinite tide behind is struggling to express itself. All these struggles and competitions are but the results of our ignorance, because we do not know the proper way to unlock the gate and let the water in. However, this infinite tide behind must express itself, for it is the cause of all manifestation.

Competitions for position or gratification are only momentary, unnecessary, and extraneous effects of ignorance. Even when all competition has ceased, this perfect nature behind will make us go forward until everyone has reached perfection. Therefore, there is no reason to believe that competition is necessary to progress. Within each of us there is the potential divinity, kept in by the locks and bars of ignorance. When knowledge breaks these bars, the God within becomes manifest.

And with this, nature's task is done, this unselfish task that our sweet nurse, nature, had imposed upon herself. She gently took the self-forgetting soul by the hand, as it were, and showed him all the experiences in the universe, all the manifestations, bringing him higher and higher through various bodies, till his lost glory came back, and he remembered his own divine nature. Then the kind mother went back the same way she came, for others who also have lost their way in the trackless desert of life. And thus, she is working, without beginning and without end. And thus, through pleasure and pain, through good and evil, the infinite river of souls is flowing into the ocean of perfection, of self-realization. Glory unto those who have realized their own nature. May their blessing be on us all!

Appendix

The 1893 World Parliament of Religions

THE WORLD'S FIRST PARLIAMENT of Religions, which was held in the city of Chicago from September 11 to 27, 1893, was one of the great epoch-making events in the history of religions, especially in regards to Hinduism. Delegates came from all parts of the world, representing every form of organized religious belief. It was not only a Parliament of Religions; it was a parliament of humanity; and if this great assembly of religious ideas and creeds had done nothing more than make society aware of the "Unity in diversity" of the religious outlook of man, it would still have been unequaled among ecumenical conventions in character and importance. But it did far more than that. It roused a wave of new awareness in the Western world of the profundity and vitality of Eastern thought.

News that the Parliament was to be held was heralded to all parts of the globe. Committees of various kinds were formed to organize it on a proper basis, and invitations were sent out to the heads or executive bodies of religious organizations the world over. Every religious creed was to send its own delegate or delegates, as the case might be, and reception committees were to receive them on their arrival in Chicago.

During the seventeen days of the Parliament proper, there assembled a great concourse of humanity, which included many of the most distinguished people of the world. Many of the greatest minds of the West were in daily attendance, and among the delegates were high ecclesiastics of various faiths.

The main sessions of the Parliament were held morning, afternoon, and evening in the large Hall of Columbus. Generally, the Hall of Columbus was full to overflowing; indeed, at times the overflow was so great that it nearly filled the adjoining twin Hall of Washington, where the speakers repeated their lectures to a second vast audience. Hundreds of papers and addresses were delivered during the main sessions. In addition, many talks were given before the thirty-five denominational congresses and auxiliary sections which were held either in the Hall of Washington or in the smaller halls of the building.

Swami Vivekananda himself described the opening of the Parliament and his own state of mind in replying to the welcome offered to the delegates:

> On the morning of the opening of the Parliament, we all assembled in a building called the Art Palace, where one huge, and other smaller temporary halls were erected for the sittings of the Parliament. People from all nations were there. There was a grand procession, and we were all marshaled onto the platform. Imagine a hall below and a huge gallery above, packed with six or seven thousand men and women representing the best culture of the country, and on the platform learned men of all nations on the earth. And I who never spoke in public in my life to address this august assemblage!
>
> It was opened in great form with music and ceremony and speeches; then the delegates were introduced one by one, and they stepped up and spoke! Of course my heart was fluttering and my tongue nearly dried up; I was so nervous, and could not venture to speak in the morning. All were prepared and came with ready-made speeches. I was a fool and had none, but stepped up and made a short speech, and when it was finished, I sat down almost exhausted with emotion.

Indeed, that sea of faces might have given even a practiced orator stage fright. To speak before such a distinguished, critical, and highly intellectual gathering required intense self-confidence. The Swami had walked in the imposing procession of delegates, and had seen the huge assembly, the eager faces of the audience, and the authoritative and dignified princes of the Christian churches who sat on the platform. He was lost in amazement by the splendor of it all.

He himself was alternately rapt in silent prayer and stirred by the eloquence of the speakers who had preceded him. Several times he had been called upon to speak, but he had said, "No, not now," until the Chairman was puzzled and wondered if he would speak at all. At length, in the late afternoon, the Chairman insisted, and the Swami arose.

His face glowed like fire. His eyes surveyed in a sweep the huge assembly before him. The whole audience grew intent; a pin could have been heard to fall. Then he addressed his audience as "Sisters and Brothers of America." And with that, before he had uttered another word, the whole Parliament was caught up in a great wave of enthusiasm, as "seven thousand people rose to their feet in tribute" with shouts of applause. The Parliament had gone mad; everyone was cheering, cheering, cheering! The Swami was bewildered. For several minutes he attempted to speak, but the wild enthusiasm of the audience prevented it.

The audience, as a whole, could not have known precisely why it cheered for Swamiji at his very first words. In other cases, there had been obvious reasons: political or religious sympathy, or previous knowledge of the speaker. In Vivekananda's case there was nothing like this. No, it was inspired by something unspoken that came through Swamiji's words. Bearing in mind that this was the first time he had addressed the great American public, and that he himself was strongly moved by the occasion, one cannot but think that the deepest powers of his Spirit were fully active as he stood there on the platform, and that the knowledge of his oneness with that huge crowd of men and women was communicating itself irresistibly to those who saw and heard him. The spontaneous and prolonged standing ovation that met Swamiji's first words of greeting sprang from a source as deep as did those words themselves, and the rapport that was immediately created between himself and his audience beckoned the real significance of his visit to the West. When silence was restored, the Swami continued his address, quoted here in part:

> It fills my heart with joy unspeakable to rise in response to the grand words of welcome given to us by you. I thank you in the name of the most ancient order of monks the world has ever seen, of which the Buddha was only a member. I thank you in the name of the Mother of religions, of which Buddhism and Jainism are but branches; and I thank you, finally, in the name of the millions and millions of Hindu people . . .
>
> I am proud to belong to a religion that has taught the world both tolerance and universal acceptance . . . We believe not only in universal tolerance but we accept all religions to be true. I will quote to you, sisters and brothers, a few lines from a hymn which every Hindu child repeats every day. I feel that the very spirit of this hymn, which I have repeated from my earliest boyhood, which is every day repeated by millions and millions of people in India, has at last come to be realized. "As the different streams, having their sources in different places, all mingle their water in the sea; O Lord, so the different paths which men take through different tendencies, various though they appear, crooked or straight, all lead to Thee."

The present convention, which is one of the most august assemblies ever held, is in itself an indication, a declaration to the world of the wonderful doctrine preached in the Bhagavad Gita: "Whosoever comes to Me, through whatsoever form I reach him, all are struggling through paths that in the end always lead to Me."

Sectarianism, bigotry and its horrible descendant, fanaticism, have possessed long this beautiful earth. It has filled the earth with violence, drenched it often and often with human blood, destroyed civilizations, and sent whole nations into despair. But its time has come, and I fervently believe that the bell that tolled this morning in honor of the representatives of the different religions of the earth at this Parliament is the death-knell to all fanaticism, that it is the death-knell to all persecution with the sword or the pen, and to all uncharitable feelings between brethren winding their way to the same goal, but through different ways.

The applause that had punctuated Swamiji's talk thundered out at its close. The people had recognized their hero and had taken him to their hearts; thenceforth he was the star of the Parliament.

It was only a short talk, but its spirit of universality, its fundamental earnestness, and its broadmindedness completely captivated the whole assembly. The Swami announced the universality of religious truths and the sameness of the goal of all religious realizations. And he was able to do so because he had sat at the feet of Paramahamsa Ramakrishna, a man of complete and authentic Realization, in far-off India, and had learned from him the truth that all religions were one, that they were all paths leading to the selfsame goal, the selfsame God. When the Swami sat down, the Parliament signified its approval by giving him a great and continuous ovation.

Commenting on the reception accorded to the Swami's first appearance before the Parliament, the Rev. John Henry Barrows wrote in *The World's Parliament of Religions,* "When Swami Vivekananda addressed the audience as 'Sisters and Brothers of America,' there arose a standing ovation that lasted for several minutes." Another eyewitness, Mrs. S. K. Blodgett, later recalled: "When that young man got up and said, 'Sisters and Brothers of America,' seven thousand people rose to their feet as a tribute to something they knew not what."

There are several contemporaneous descriptions and appreciations of Swamiji quoted in *Life Magazine,* and from various periodicals such as the *Boston Evening Transcript.* One of the finest appraisals comes from the Honorable Mr. Merwin-Marie Snell, President of the Scientific Section of the Parliament, as reported in *Life Magazine;*

> Vivekananda was beyond question the most popular and influential speaker in the Parliament, who on all occasions was received with greater enthusiasm than any other speaker, Christian or Pagan.

Harriet Monroe, the founder of *Poetry: A Magazine of Verse,* a publication through which she introduced many of America's now famous poets, attended the World's Fair, and recorded her impressions of the Parliament and of Vivekananda:

> The Congress of Religions was a triumph for all concerned, especially for its generalissimo, the Reverend John H. Barrows, of Chicago's First Presbyterian Church, who had been preparing it for two years. When he brought down his gavel upon the world's first

Parliament of Religions, a wave of breathless silence swept over the audience — it seemed a great moment in human history, prophetic of the promised new era of tolerance and peace. On the stage with him, at his left, was a black-coated array of bishops and ministers representing the various familiar Protestant sects and the Russian Orthodox and Roman Catholic Churches; at his right, a brilliant group of strangely costumed dignitaries from afar — a Confucian from China, a Jain from India, a Theosophist from Allahabad, a white-robed Shinto priest and four Buddhists from Japan, and a monk of the orange robe from Bombay.

It was the last of these, Swami Vivekananda, the magnificent, who stole the whole show and captured the town. Others of the foreign groups spoke well, but the handsome monk in the orange robe gave us in perfect English a masterpiece. His personality, dominant, magnetic; his voice, rich as a bronze bell; the controlled fervor of his feeling; the beauty of his message to the Western world he was facing for the first time — these combined to give us a rare and perfect moment of supreme emotion. It was human eloquence at its highest pitch.

On September 19, the Swami read his celebrated paper on "Hinduism" — a summary of the philosophy, psychology, and general ideas and practices of Hinduism. Though the Swami was not the only Indian, or even the only Bengali present, he was the only representative of Hinduism proper. The other Hindu delegates stood for societies or churches or sects, but the Swami stood for Hinduism in its universal aspect. He gave forth the ideas of the Hindus concerning the soul and its destiny; he expounded the doctrines of the Vedanta philosophy, which harmonizes all religious ideals and all forms of worship, viewing them as various presentations of truth and as various paths to its realization. He preached the religious philosophy of Hinduism, which declares the soul to be eternally pure, eternally free, only appearing in the material world of the senses to be limited and manifold. He spoke of the attainment of the goal — the realization of One Eternal Divinity — as the result of innumerable efforts of many lives. He said that in order to realize our own Divinity, the self that says "I" and "mine" must vanish. This, however, did not mean the denial of true individuality; it meant, rather, its utmost fulfillment. By destroying the ignorance of selfishness within, one attained to infinite, universal individuality. The pervasive spirit of his address was the truth of Oneness. And he insisted that the realization of the Divinity within us inevitably led to our being able to see Divinity manifest everywhere.

In this stunning talk, Swami Vivekananda gave coherence and unity to the bewildering number of sects and beliefs that through untold ages have gathered and flowered under the name of Hinduism. He revealed the central beliefs common to each widely divergent sect. He made it all not only clear but supremely inspiring, a living religion springing eternally from the very soul of humanity itself.

Indeed, in this first statement of the Hindu religion that Swamiji made to the American public lay the seeds of all his subsequent teachings; that which he was later to develop and formulate in language adapted to Western understanding and culture was all there. Perhaps in that moment not only was Hinduism re-created, but a new religion for the world was given its first enunciation in the West — a religion both fulfilling the past, and lighting up the future.

Among the many people who long remembered Swamiji's paper on Hinduism and were profoundly moved by it, was a young student who went on to become a well-known and influential philosopher. In his "Recollections of Swami Vivekananda," William Ernest Hocking wrote in his later years:

> We all carry about with us unsolved problems of adjustment to this many-angled world. Without formulating questions, we are living quests, unless by some rare chance our philosophy of life is entirely settled. And to meet such a person may resolve a quest wholly without his knowledge; it may simply be a mode of being that brings the release.
>
> This was in measure the story of my first encounter with Swami Vivekananda, though I was only one of an immense audience . . . I was a casual visitor at the Fair, just turning twenty, interested in a dozen exhibits on the Midway . . . But aside from all this, I had a quietly disturbing problem of my own.
>
> I had been reading all I could get of the works of Herbert Spencer . . . I was convinced by him; . . . and yet it was somehow a vital injury to think of man as merely of the animals — birth, growth, mating, death — and nothing more — finis. I had had in my religion — Methodism — an experience of conversion with a strange enlightenment that gave me three days of what felt like a new vision of things, strangely lifted up. Spencer had explained that all away as just an emotional flurry — the world must be faced with a steady objective eye. The Christian cosmology was simply fancy.
>
> But still, Christianity was not the only religion. There were to be speakers from other traditions. They might have some insight that would relieve the tension. I would go for an hour and listen. I didn't know the program. It happened to be Vivekananda's period.

He spoke not as arguing from a tradition, or from a book, but as from an experience and certitude of his own. I do not recall the steps of his address. But there was a passage toward the end, in which I can still hear the ring of his voice, and feel the silence of the crowd — almost as if shocked. The audience was well-mixed, but could be taken as one in assuming the Christian teachings that there had been a "fall of man" resulting in a state of "original sin," such that "All men have sinned and come short of the glory of God." But what is the speaker saying? I hear his emphatic rebuke:

"Call men sinners?
It is a sin to call men sinners!"

Through the silence I felt something like a gasp running through the hall as the audience waited for the affirmation which must follow this blow. What his following words were, I cannot recall with the same verbal clarity: they carried the message that in all men there is that divine essence, undivided and eternal: reality is One, and that One, which is Brahman, constitutes the central being of each one of us.

For me, this doctrine was a startling departure from anything that my scientific psychology could then recognize. One must live with these ideas and consider how one's inner experience could entertain them. But what I could feel and understand was that this man was speaking from what he knew, not from what he had been told. He was well aware of the books; but he was more immediately aware of his own experience and his own status in the world; and what he said would have to be taken into account in any final world-view. I began to realize that Spencer could not be allowed the last word. And furthermore, that this religious experience of mine, which Spencer would dismiss as a psychological flurry, was very akin to the grounds of Vivekananda's own certitude.

Day after day the Parliament went on, with the Swami often speaking extemporaneously at its main sessions. He was allowed to speak longer than the usual half-hour, and being the most popular speaker, he was always scheduled last in order to hold the audience. The people would sit from ten in the morning to ten at night, with only a recess of a half-hour for lunch, listening to paper after paper, in order to hear their favorite.

On September 27, the Swami delivered his "Address at the Final Session," and here he again rose to one of his most prophetic and luminous moods. He declared:

The Christian is not to become a Hindu or a Buddhist, nor a Hindu or a Buddhist to become a Christian. But each must assimilate the spirit of the others, and yet preserve his individuality and grow according to his own law of growth....

If the Parliament of Religions has shown anything to the world, it is this: It has proved to the world that holiness, purity, and charity are not the exclusive possessions of any church in the world, and that every system has produced men and women of the most exalted character.

Thus did the unknown monk blossom into a world figure; the wandering renunciate of solitary days in India had overnight become the Prophet of a New Dispensation!

On all sides his name resounded. Life-size pictures of him were posted in the streets of Chicago, with the words "The Monk Vivekananda" beneath them, and passers-by would stop to do reverence with bowed head. "From the day the wonderful Professor (Vivekananda) delivered his speech, which was followed by other addresses, he was followed by a crowd wherever he went," a contemporary newspaper reported. The press rang with his fame. The best known and most conservative of the metropolitan newspapers proclaimed him a Prophet and a Seer. Indeed, the *New York Herald* spoke of him in these words:

He is undoubtedly the greatest figure in the Parliament of Religions. After hearing him we feel how foolish it is to send missionaries to this learned nation.

The *Boston Evening Transcript* wrote on September 30:

He is a great favorite at the Parliament from the grandeur of his sentiments and his appearance as well. If he merely crosses the platform he is applauded, and yet this marked approval of thousands he accepts in a child-like spirit of gratification without a trace of conceit.

Other leading newspapers of the United States were also eloquent about Swami Vivekananda. Well-known periodicals quoted his talks in full. The *Review of Reviews* described his address as "noble and sublime," and the *Critic* of New York spoke of him as "an orator by Divine right." Similar accounts of the Swami's triumph appeared in other papers too numerous to quote here.

Among personal appreciations, the Honorable Merwin-Marie Snell wrote some time after:

No religious body made so profound an impression upon the Parliament and the American people at large as did Hinduism. And by far the most important representative of Hinduism was Swami Vivekananda, who, in fact, was beyond question the most popular and influential man in the Parliament. He frequently spoke, both on the floor of the Parliament itself, and at the meetings of the Scientific Section over which I had the honor to preside, and, on all occasions, he was received with greater enthusiasm than any other speaker, Christian or "Pagan." The people thronged about him wherever he went, and hung with eagerness on his every word . . . The most rigid of orthodox Christians say of him, "He is indeed a prince among men!"

Dr. Annie Besant, who helped popularize the movement of Theosophy, gave her impression of the Swami at the Parliament:

A striking figure, clad in yellow and orange, shining like the sun of India in the midst of the heavy atmosphere of Chicago, a lion head, piercing eyes, mobile lips, movements swift and abrupt — such was my first impression of Swami Vivekananda, as I met him in one of the rooms set apart for the use of the delegates to the Parliament of Religions. Off the platform, his figure was instinct with pride of country, pride of race — the representative of the oldest of living religions, surrounded by curious gazers of nearly the youngest religion. India was not to be shamed before the hurrying arrogant West by this her envoy and her son. He brought her message, he spoke in her name, and the herald remembered the dignity of the royal land whence he came. Purposeful, virile, strong, he stood out, a man among men, able to hold his own.

On the platform another side came out. The dignity and the inborn sense of worth and power still were there, but all was subdued to the exquisite beauty of the spiritual message which he had brought, to the sublimity of that matchless truth of the East which is the heart and the life of India, the wondrous teaching of the Self. Enraptured, the huge multitude hung upon his words; not a syllable must be lost, not a cadence missed! "That man, a heathen!" said one, as he came out of the great hall, "and we send missionaries to his people! It would be more fitting that they should send missionaries to us!"

So meteoric was the transformation of the Swami from obscurity to fame, that it can be truly said that he "awoke one morning to find himself famous."

Though the news about the proceedings of the Parliament of Religions, and about the Swami, had been coming out in the Indian newspapers since mid-September of 1893, it did not catch the attention of the Indian people till November, when a long article entitled "Hindus at the Fair," first published in the *Boston Evening Transcript* of September 23, appeared in the leading papers of Bombay, Calcutta, and Madras. This article brought to India the first inkling that something extraordinary was taking place halfway around the globe. It read in part:

Vivekananda's address before the Parliament was broad as the heavens above us; embracing the best in all religions, as the ultimate universal religion — charity to all mankind, good works for the love of God, not for fear of punishment or hope of reward. He is a great favorite at the Parliament, from the grandeur of his sentiments and his appearance as well. If he merely crosses the platform he is applauded, and this marked approval of thousands he accepts in a childlike spirit of gratification, without a tram of conceit. It must be a strange experience, too, for this humble young Brahmin monk, this sudden transition from poverty and self-effacement, to affluence and aggrandizement . . .

From that time on, as news of Swami Vivekananda's spectacular success at Chicago came from the American Press, it was reprinted in the leading Indian newspapers, notably the *Indian Mirror,* with enthusiastic editorial comments. It was not long before all of India knew that a young monk, a penniless *sannyasin,* had crossed the ocean, mixed with foreigners, and conquered the great international Parliament of Religions.

Soon after came the publication of the Rev. John Henry Barrows' two-volume work, *The World's Parliament of Religions* — an official and detailed history of the event. The book was reviewed exhaustively in the January issue of the American periodical the *Review of Reviews,* which account was, in turn, commented upon at length in an editorial in the *Indian Mirror* of February 21, 1894. The fact that Barrows had given a prominent place to Swami Vivekananda and to his paper on Hinduism in his history put an official and impressive seal on the Swami's great accomplishment. His achievement could no longer be brushed aside as a passing sensation by Christian missionaries and others to whose interest it was to discredit him. The deep mark he had made was now a matter of solid historical record. The *Mirror's* editorial read in part:

Dr. John Henry Barrows, the President of the Parliament of Religions, has just published the official report of the Parliament. A prominent place has been accorded to Swami Vivekananda in the report. "This speaker," says Dr. Barrows, "is a high-caste Hindu and representative of orthodox Hinduism. He was one of the principal personalities in the Parliament." Dr. Barrows characterizes the Swami's address as "noble and sublime," and it was so much appreciated for its breadth, its sincerity and its excellent spirit of toleration, that the Hindu representative soon came to be as much liked outside the Parliament as within it . . .

Whatever may be the practical outcome of Swami Vivekananda's mission to America, there can be no question that it has already had the effect of immensely raising the credit of true Hinduism in the eyes of the civilized world, and that is, indeed, a work for which the whole Hindu community should feel grateful to the Swami.

Mr. Merwin-Marie Snell, President of the Scientific Section of the Parliament, wrote a long letter to the editor of the *Pioneer*, an Anglo-Indian newspaper of Allahabad. His letter, dated January 30, 1894, was printed in the *Pioneer* on March 8 of the same year.

This laudatory letter, written by a highly respected Western scholar, together with editorial reactions to it, added to India's amazement and journalistic attention relating to the Swami's success at the Parliament of Religions. A passage from Mr. Snell's letter has been quoted earlier in this chapter; other portions read as follows:

I have felt inspired to voice the unanimous and heart-felt gratitude and appreciation of the cultured and broadminded portion of our public, and to give my personal testimony, as the President of the Scientific Section of the Parliament and of all the Conferences connected with the latter, and therefore an eyewitness, to the esteem in which Paramahamsa Vivekananda is held here, the influence that he is wielding, and the good that he is doing . . .

Intense is the astonished admiration which the personal presence and bearing and language of Vivekananda have wrung from a public accustomed to think of Hindus, thanks to the fables and half-truths of the missionaries, as ignorant and degraded "heathen": there is no doubt that the continued interest is largely due to a genuine hunger for the spiritual truths which India through him has offered to the American people . . .

Never before has so authoritative a representative of genuine Hinduism, as opposed to the emasculated and Anglicized versions of it so common in these days, been accessible to American inquirers: and it is certain that the American people at large, will, when he is gone, look forward with eagerness to his return . . . America thanks India for sending him.

Mr. Snell's letter was widely circulated, and thus the Swami's achievement, confirmed again and again by highly reputable sources, was becoming deeply impressed upon the mind of the Indian people.

The next wave of amazement over the impact of Vivekananda at the Parliament of Religions to sweep over India was the publication in Madras and Calcutta of the text of the Swami's paper on "Hinduism," which he had delivered on September 19, 1893. The Calcutta pamphlet was distributed on March 11, 1894, at Dakshineswar, on the birthday celebration of

Sri Ramakrishna. The Swami's address created perhaps the greatest sensation of all, for it left no doubt of what precisely he had said to the American people, and in what precisely his achievement consisted. On March 21, the *Indian Mirror* printed a lengthy excerpt from his paper, commenting in part:

> The spirit that reigned over the Parliament and dominated the soul of almost every religious representative present was that of universal toleration and universal deliverance, and it ought to be a matter of pride to India, to all Hindus specially, that no one expressed, as the American papers say, this spirit so well as the Hindu representative, Swami Vivekananda. His address struck the keynote of the Parliament of Religions . . . The spirit of catholicity and toleration which distinguishes Hinduism, forming one of its broadest features, was never before so prominently brought to the notice of the world as it has been by Swami Vivekananda, and we make no doubt that the Swami's address will have an effect on other religions, whose teachers, preachers, and missionaries heard him, and were impressed by his utterances.

As the Swami's "Paper on Hinduism" circulated through India, the tremendous historical significance of his mission became apparent to all. His epoch-making representation of Hinduism at the Parliament was to raise India not only in the estimation of the West, but in her own estimation as well, and was eventually to bring about a profound change in her national life. Years later, on the Swami's passing from this world, the *Brahmavadin* commented:

Had the late lamented Swami Vivekananda done nothing more than attend the Parliament of Religions in Chicago and deliver that one speech that brought India and America together almost immediately, he would still have been entitled to our fullest gratitude. That speech compelled attention both in method and substance. To Swami Vivekananda belongs the undying honor of being the pioneer in the noble work of Hindu religious revival.

The Swami's appearance at the Parliament of Religions had without question made him irreversibly famous throughout the world. Never again was he to wander alone, unknown through his beloved country. His world mission in its public aspect had begun. But in the midst of all the immediate acclaim and popularity that his appearance at the Parliament had brought him, he had no thought for himself; his heart continued to bleed for the impoverished in India. Personally he had no more wants. The mansions of some of the wealthiest of Chicago society were open to him, and he was received as an honored guest. But instead of feeling happy in this splendid environment, his heart continued to cry for the suffering souls in his beloved India. Name and fame and the approval of thousands had in no way affected him; though sumptuously cared for, he was the same monk as of old, always thinking of India's poor. As he retired the first night and lay upon his bed, the terrible contrast between poverty-stricken India and opulent America pressed on him. He could not sleep for pondering over India's plight. At length, overcome with emotion, he cried, "O Mother, to what a sad pass have we poor Indians come when millions of us die for want of a handful of rice, and here they spend millions of rupees upon their personal comforts! Who will raise the masses in India! Who will give them bread? Show me, O Mother, how I can help them."

Over and over again one finds the same intense love for the suffering shining out in his words and actions. The deep and spontaneous love that welled in his heart for the poor, the distressed, and the despised was the inexhaustible spring of all his activities. From this point on, Swami's life becomes a world of intense thought and work. Hand in hand with giving the message of Hinduism to the West, the Swami was to work constantly trying to solve the problems of his country. Though the dusty roads and the parched tongue and the hunger of his days as a wandering monk were ascetic in the extreme, the experiences he was to undergo in foreign lands were to be even more severe. He was to strain himself to the utmost. He was to work until work was no longer possible and the body dropped off from sheer exhaustion.

(From *The Life of Swami Vivekananda* and *Swami Vivekananda in the West*)

Vivekananda: A Biography

SWAMI VIVEKANANDA WAS BORN Narendranath Datta on January 12, 1863. The Datta family was wealthy and respectable, and renowned for their charity, education, and strong spirit of independence. Naren's grandfather was well versed in Persian and Sanskrit, and was skilled in law, but after the birth of his son, he renounced the world and became a monk. He was then only twenty-five years of age.

Naren's father, Vishwanath Datta, was an attorney-at-law in the Calcutta High Court. He was proficient in English and Persian, and took great delight in reciting to his family the poems of the Persian poet Hafiz. He also enjoyed the study of the Bible, and of the Hindu scriptures in Sanskrit. Charitable to an extravagant degree in sympathy for the poor, Vishwanath had a rationalistic as well as progressive outlook in religious and social matters, owing perhaps to the influence of Western culture. Naren's mother, Bhuvaneshwari Devi, was a deeply religious and accomplished lady, with a regal bearing.

In his early childhood, Naren had a great attraction for spiritual matters, and would play at worshiping or meditating on the images of Rama-Sita, Shiva, and others. The revered spiritual stories of the *Ramayana* and the *Mahabharata,* which his mother taught him, left an indelible impression on his mind. Traits such as courage, sympathy for the poor, and attraction towards wandering monks appeared spontaneously in him. Yet even in childhood, Naren demanded convincing arguments for every proposition. With these qualities of head *and* heart, he grew into a vigorous youth.

As a youth, Naren's leonine beauty was matched by his courage. He had the build of an athlete, a resonant voice, and a brilliant intellect. He distinguished himself in athletics and music, and among his colleagues he was the undisputed leader. At college he studied and absorbed Western thought, and this implanted a spirit of critical inquiry in his mind. His rational mind and sharp intellect were now at war with his inborn tendency towards spirituality and his respect for ancient religious traditions and beliefs. In this predicament, he tried to find inspiration in the Brahmo Samaj, the popular socio-religious movement of the time. The Brahmo Samaj believed in a formless God, denounced the worship of idols, and addressed itself to various forms of social reform. Naren also met prominent religious leaders, but could not get a convincing answer from them to his questions about the existence of God. This only accentuated his spiritual restlessness.

At this critical juncture, he remembered the words of one of his professors, who had mentioned that a saint lived at Dakshineswar, just outside Calcutta, who had experienced the ecstasy described by Wordsworth in his poem *The Excursion*. Thus came about, in 1881, the historic meeting of these two great souls; Ramakrishna, the great prophet of modern India, and the future Vivekananda, the carrier of his message. Naren asked, "Sir, have you seen God?" Sri Ramakrishna answered his question in the affirmative, "Yes, I have seen Him just as I see you here, only more intensely." At last, here was one who could assure him from his own *experience* that God existed and could be realized. The disciple's training had begun.

While Sri Ramakrishna tested him in so many ways, Naren in turn tested Sri Ramakrishna in order to ascertain the truth of his spiritual assertions. Gradually, Naren surrendered himself to the Master. And Sri Ramakrishna, with infinite patience, calmed the rebellious spirit of his young disciple, and led him forth from doubt to certainty, and from anguish to spiritual bliss. But, more than Sri Ramakrishna's spiritual guidance and support, it was his love which conquered young Naren, love which the disciple reciprocated in full measure.

With Sri Ramakrishna's illness in 1885 came his removal from Dakshineswar to Cossipore for treatment; and so began Naren's final training under his Guru. It was a time remarkable for the intense spiritual fire which burned within him, and which expressed itself through various intense practices. Ramakrishna utilized the opportunity to bring his young disciples under the leadership of Naren. Three or four days before his passing, Sri Ramakrishna transmitted to Naren his own power, and told him, "By the force of the power transmitted by me, great things will be done by you."

After the passing away of the Master in August 1886, many of the young disciples gathered together in an old dilapidated house at Baranagore, under the leadership of Naren. Here, in the midst of a life of intense austerity and spiritual practices, the foundation of the Ramakrishna brotherhood was laid. It was during these days that Naren, along with many of his brother disciples, took the vow of *sannyasa*, renunciation. The days at Baranagore were full of great joy, study, and spiritual practices. But the call of the wandering life of the *sannyasin* was now felt by most of the monks. And Naren, too, towards the close of 1888, began to take temporary excursions away from the monastery.

The Wandering Monk

A remarkable change of outlook came over Naren between the end of 1888, when he first left on his temporary excursions, and 1890, when he parted from his brethren and traveled alone as an unknown mendicant. He began to assume various names in order to conceal his identity, that he might be swallowed up in the immensity of India.

Now the natural desire of an Indian monk for a life of solitude gave way to the understanding that he was to fulfil a great destiny; that his was not the life of an ordinary monk struggling for personal salvation. In July 1890, under the influence of his burning desire to know India better and the appeal rising all around him from oppressed India, the Swami took leave of his brother monks with the firm resolve to cut himself free from all ties and to go into the solitude of the Himalayas. In the words of Romain Rolland, "This was the great departure. Like a diver he plunged into the Ocean of India and the Ocean of India covered his tracks." Among its countless people he was nothing more than one nameless monk in saffron robe among a thousand others. But the fires of genius burned in his eyes. He was a prince despite all disguise.

His wanderings took him to various places of pilgrimage and historical interest. Everywhere he went, the glory of ancient India vividly came before his eyes, whether political, cultural, or spiritual. In the midst of this great education, the abject misery of the Indian masses stood out before his mind. He moved from one princely State to another, everywhere trying to find ways to relieve the suffering of the poor. Thus he came to meet many leading personalities and rulers of the princely States. Among them was the Maharaja of Mysore, who gave him the financial support necessary to travel to the West to seek help for India, and to preach the eternal religion to the modern world.

Wherever he went, the terrible poverty and misery of the masses caused his soul to burn in agony. He had traveled through the whole of India, often on foot, for nearly three years, coming to know India first hand. Now he had reached the southern tip of India. The vast panorama of his experiences during his travels passed before his mind's eye. He meditated on the past, the present, and the future of India, on the causes of her downfall, and the means of her resurrection. He then made the momentous decision to go to the West to seek help for the poor of India, and thus gave shape to his life's mission.

With this decision, he journeyed on to Madras, where a group of young men were eagerly awaiting his arrival. To them he revealed his intention of visiting America to attend the Parliament of Religions that was being convened at Chicago. His young disciples forthwith raised a subscription for his passage. At this juncture, the Swami had a symbolic vision in which Sri Ramakrishna walked out into the sea and beckoned him to follow. This, coupled with the blessings of Sri Ramakrishna's holy consort, Sri Sarada Devi, settled the question for him. His journey to America commenced on May 31, 1893.

On the World Stage

Swami Vivekananda traveled to America at the young age of thirty, reaching Chicago in July of 1893. To his disappointment, he learned that the Parliament of Religions would not be held until September, and, worse, that no one could be a delegate without credentials! Resigning himself to the will of Providence, he went to Boston, where he was told it was less expensive to stay. On the train to Boston, he happened to become acquainted with Miss Katherine Sanborn, who invited him to be her guest in Boston. Through her he came to know Professor John Henry Wright of Harvard University, who gave him a letter of introduction to the Chairman of the Parliament of Religions. In the course of this letter, Dr. Wright said, "Here is a man who is more learned than all our learned professors put together."

The Swami returned to Chicago a couple of days before the opening of the Parliament of Religions, but found to his dismay that he had lost the address of the committee that was providing hospitality for the Oriental delegates. After a night's rest in a boxcar in the railway freight yard, the Swami set out in the morning to find somebody who could help him out of this difficulty. But help for a dark-skinned Indian man in 1893 America was not readily available. Exhausted by a fruitless search, he sat down on the roadside, resigning himself once again to the divine will. Suddenly, a lady of regal appearance emerged from a fashionable house across the street, approached him, and offered him help. This was Mrs. George W. Hale, whose house was to become the permanent address of the Swami while in the United States, for the Hale family became his devoted followers.

The Parliament of Religions opened in September of 1893. The spacious hall of the Art Institute was packed with thousands of people representing the best culture of the country. On the platform every organized religion from all corners of the world had its representative. The Swami had never addressed such a huge and distinguished gathering. When his turn came, he mentally bowed down to Sarasvati, the goddess of learning, and then began his address with the words, "Sisters and Brothers of America." Immediately there was thunderous applause from the vast audience, and it lasted for a full two minutes. The appeal of his simple words of burning sincerity, his great personality, and his bright countenance were so great that the next day the newspapers described him as the greatest figure in the Parliament of Religions. The simple monk with a begging bowl had become the man of the hour.

All the subsequent speeches of the Swami at the Parliament were listened to with great respect and appreciation. They all had one common theme — universality. While all the delegates to the Parliament spoke of their own religion, the Swami spoke of a religion that was vast as the sky and deep as the ocean.

When the Parliament ended, the days of quiet had ended for the Swami. What followed were days of hectic lecturing in almost every part of the United States. Having signed a contract for a lecture tour with a bureau, the Swami had to be constantly on the move, speaking to all sorts of audiences. He lectured in most of the larger cities of the eastern, midwestern, and southern states, including Chicago, Iowa City, Des Moines, Memphis, Indianapolis, Minneapolis, Madison, Detroit, Hartford, Buffalo, Boston, Cambridge, Baltimore, Washington, Brooklyn, and New York.

Swami used the lecture tour to acquire funds in order to help relieve the suffering and poverty in India, as well as to bring to the West the ancient Indian wisdom of Vedanta and practices of Classical Yoga. He had decided to earn money for India only through his own labor, without appealing publicly for contributions. Of course, as a renunciate and monk, not a penny ever went to Vivekananda himself.

This first stay in America, which was to last more than three years, was packed with intense activity. Though the lecture tour provided him with opportunities of knowing the different aspects of Western life first hand, he wanted to form a group of earnest American disciples, and so he eventually left the lecture bureau and began classes, free of charge, for sincere students. Besides giving numerous lectures and classes in New York during this time, he founded the first Vedanta Society in America there. He also trained a group of close disciples at Thousand Island Park, wrote *Raja Yoga*, and paid two successful visits to England, where he gave the lectures which now form *Jnana Yoga*. The results of his work produced such an impression that he was offered the Chair of Eastern Philosophy at both Harvard University and Columbia University.

He had labored hard to give to the West his message of Vedanta as the universal principle basic to all religions, and his efforts had by now resulted in the establishment of the first center for Yoga work on a permanent basis in the United States. But his motherland was calling him, eager to receive his message, and so, at the end of 1896, he returned to India. Besides his American disciples, he left behind his brother disciples Saradananda and Abhedananda to carry on the work.

Triumphal Return

Swami Vivekananda left for India in December of 1896. The news of the Swami's return had already reached India, and people everywhere throughout the country were afire with enthusiasm to receive him. At Madras he delivered public lectures, every one of which was a clarion call to rise to build a new India. He emphasized that in India, "the keynote of the whole music of the national life" was religion, a religion which preached the "spiritual oneness of the whole universe," and that when that religion was strengthened, everything else would take care of itself. He did not spare his criticism, however, castigating his countrymen for their blind adherence to old superstitions, for their caste prejudices, and so on.

From Madras the Swami traveled to Calcutta, and arrived there in February of 1897. His native city gave him a grand welcome, and here the Swami paid a touching tribute to his Master, Paramahamsa Ramakrishna:

> If there has been anything achieved by me, if from my lips has ever fallen one word that has helped anyone in the world, I lay no claim to it; it was his. If this nation wants to rise, take my word for it, it will have to rally around his name.

To establish Ramakrishna's work on a firm basis, Vivekananda, along with all the monastic and lay disciples, formed the Ramakrishna Mission in May of 1897. The aims and ideals of the Mission propounded by the Swami were purely spiritual and humanitarian. He had inaugurated the machinery for carrying out his ideas.

In January 1899, the monks moved to a new monastery, the now famous Belur Math. The Nivedita Girls' School had been inaugurated earlier. The Bengali monthly *Udbodhan* was also started at this time. And the Seviers, two of Vivekananda's Western disciples, fulfilled the Swami's dream of having a monastery in the Himalayas by starting the Advaita Ashrama at Mayavati, Pithoragarh, in March 1899.

During this period, the Swami constantly inspired the *sannyasins* and *brahmacharins* at the Math towards a life of intense spirituality and service, for one's own emancipation and the good of one's fellow men — *Atmano mokshartham jagadhitaya cha*, as he put it. But the Swami's health was failing. So his plan to revisit the West was welcomed by his brother monks in the hope that this would improve his health.

Across the World Again

Swami Vivekananda left India in June of 1899. After spending two weeks in London, he sailed for New York. Arriving there, he stayed at Ridgely Manor, on the Hudson River, until November, when he went to the West Coast.

The Swami traveled and lectured extensively on the West Coast until June of 1900. He compensated, as it were, for his omission of the West Coast during his earlier visit. His work during this period was of a tremendous magnitude and significance. Some of his most famous lectures were delivered during this period. Great enthusiasm was created in the cities of Los Angeles, San Francisco, Pasadena, Alameda, and Oakland. The Swami's health had improved after the sea-voyage, and once again he poured out his soul in giving his great message to the American people.

Now the conviction that the East and the West ought to be mutually helpful and cooperate with each other grew stronger within him. The mere material brilliance of the West could not dazzle him, nor could the emphasis on spirituality in India hide her social and economic drawbacks. Now East and West must work hand in hand for the good of each other, without destroying the special characteristics of each. The West has much to learn from the East, and the East has much to learn from the West: in fact, the future has to be shaped by a proper fusion of the two ideals. Then there will be neither East nor West, but one humanity.

During this time, Swami founded the Vedanta Center of San Francisco, and the Shanti Ashrama in Northern California was opened. In spite of tremendous activity, the Swami was becoming more and more aware of the approaching end. In April of 1900, he wrote to one of his disciples: "My boat is nearing the calm harbor from which it is never more to be driven out."

In August of 1900, he arrived in Paris to participate in the Congress of the History of Religions. He left Paris in October, and went on to visit Hungary, Rumania, Serbia, Bulgaria, Constantinople, Athens, and Cairo. In Cairo, the Swami suddenly became restless to return home. He took the first available boat to India, and reached the Belur Math in December of 1900. It was a surprise to his brother monks and disciples, who greatly rejoiced at his return.

The Journey's End

Returning to Belur Math, the Swami tried to lead a carefree life at the monastery. He would roam about the Math grounds, sometimes clad only in his loin-cloth; or he would supervise the cooking; or he would sit with the monks singing devotional songs. Sometimes he would be seen imparting spiritual instruction to visitors, at other times engaged in serious study in his room or explaining to the members of the Math the intricate passages of the scriptures.

Towards the end of 1901, he went to Varanasi, where he was delighted to see how some young men, inspired by his call to service, had started nursing the poor and the needy. Their work formed the nucleus of the future Ramakrishna Mission Home of Service.

The Swami knew his end was nearing. All his actions during the last days were deliberate. He said that smaller plants cannot grow under the shade of a big tree. On July 4, 1902, he meditated from 8 to 11 in the morning. In the afternoon, he went out for a walk, and in the evening, he retired to his room and spent an hour in meditation. Then he lay down quietly, and, after some time, took two deep breaths and passed into eternal rest. His followers lived to see the truth of the words he uttered not long before about his future: "It may be that I shall find it good to get outside my body — to cast it off like a worn-out garment. But I shall not cease to work. I shall inspire men everywhere, until the world shall know that it is one with God."

(From *Vivekananda: A Biography in Pictures*.)

Glossary of Terms

Advaita: Literally "not two." The Vedanta school of non-dualism that teaches the Oneness of all.

Ahimsa: Non-harmfulness in word, thought, and deed.

Akasha: The subtle substrate of all material existence. Everything that has form is evolved out of Akasha.

Ananda: Absolute, undifferentiated Bliss, beyond the duality of pain and pleasure.

Asana: Posture. The third of the eight steps of Raja Yoga.

Atman: The Supreme Soul; the One Existence indwelling, the Self. *Atman* is used interchangeably with *Brahman* in referring to the One Ultimate Existence.

Avatar: An Incarnation of God.

Bhagavad Gita: The revered Hindu scripture in which Lord Krishna teaches Arjuna the great spiritual truths and Yoga pathways to union with God.

Bhakta: A follower of Bhakti Yoga; a devotee of a Personal God.

Bhakti Yoga: One of the four Classical Yogas. The path of union through devotion to and love of a Personal God.

Brahman: The One Infinite Existence of the non-dualistic Advaita Vedanta philosophy; Sat-Chit-Ananda, Existence, Consciousness, and Bliss Absolute. The One Reality.

Chit: Absolute, undifferentiated Consciousness. Also referred to as Infinite Knowledge.

Dharana: The sixth of the eight steps of Raja Yoga, meaning concentration, the fixing of the mind upon one point alone, to the exclusion of all else.

Dhyana: The seventh of the eight steps of Raja Yoga, meaning meditation, the unbroken contemplation of the object of concentration.

Gayatri: The holiest mantra from the Vedas, recited daily by Hindus: "I meditate on the glory of that Being who has produced this universe; may He enlighten my mind."

Gita: See *Bhagavad Gita*.

Gunas: The three qualities, or energies, that make up everything in the material universe: *Tamas*, inertia and ignorance; *Rajas*, activity and passion; and *Sattva*, purity and illumination.

Guru: Literally, "slayer of darkness"; a spiritual teacher and guide.

Impersonal God: The One Infinite Existence. Brahman, the One Absolute Reality beyond qualities or form.

Ishta: The "Chosen Ideal," or "Chosen Deity." The form of God that the devotee prefers to worship or contemplate.

Ishvara: The Personal God. The greatest manifestation of impersonal Brahman possible within the limitations of time, space, and causation. The supreme Creator, Sustainer, and Dissolver of the Universe.

Jnana Yoga: One of the four Classical Yogas. The path of union with God through knowledge and intellectual discrimination.

Jnani: A follower of Jnana Yoga.

Karma: Action or work; but within Vedanta philosophy, *Karma* chiefly refers to the effects or consequences of actions or work.

Karma Yoga: One of the four Classical Yogas. The path of union with God through selfless and God-dedicated action.

Krishna: The Incarnation of God who teaches the great spiritual truths and Yoga pathways to Arjuna in the Bhagavad Gita.

Mantra: The name of God given to a disciple from his or her spiritual teacher during initiation. Also, a holy word, verse, or hymn from the Vedas.

Maya: The illusion of name and form that hides the underlying Unity of Existence.

Mukti: Liberation from the bondage of matter through union with God. Spiritual freedom, the ultimate goal of human life.

Narada: A saint in Hindu mythology.

Niyama: The second of the eight steps of Raja Yoga, made up of five observances, or virtues, that the devotee is called upon to practice and perfect.

Om: The most sacred word of the Vedas. It is the symbol of both the Personal God and of the Absolute.

Para-Bhakti: Supreme love of a Personal God.

Patanjali: The author of the Yoga Sutras, the scripture of Raja Yoga.

Personal God: God with attributes and qualities.

Prakriti: Undifferentiated nature, from which all things material arise, consisting of the three Gunas: Sattva, Rajas, and Tamas.

Prana: The primal energy. The essential substrate of all forms of energy. The infinite, omnipresent manifesting power of this universe.

Pranayama: Control of the Prana, the primal energy, manifesting in humans as breath; the fourth of the eight steps of Raja Yoga.

Pratyahara: The discipline of withdrawing the mind and internal sense organs from external sense objects; the fifth of the eight steps of Raja Yoga.

Rajas: One of the three primal qualities, or energies, that make up nature; the force of activity and passion. See *Gunas*.

Raja Yoga: One of the four Classical Yogas, taught by Patanjali in his Yoga Sutras.

Raja Yogi: A devotee who follows the practices of Raja Yoga.

Ramakrishna: The Bengali Saint (1836–1886), who is considered by millions to be an Incarnation of God. The spiritual teacher of Swami Vivekananda, whose life and message inspired the revival of Yoga and Vedanta in the modern world.

Rig-Veda: One of the four Vedas. See *Vedas*.

Rishi: A seer of Truth; a sage.

Samadhi: The superconscious state in which the ultimate union with God is achieved.

Samskara: Mental impressions, created through thoughts or actions, that become tendencies through repetition, and, over time, harden into the habits that make up character.

Samyama: The practice of the last three steps of Raja Yoga, one following the other, upon a particular object of contemplation. Concentration (Dharana), meditation (Dhyana), and absorption (Samadhi).

Sankhya: One of the six systems of orthodox Hindu philosophy.

Sannyasa: The vow of renunciation of all worldly position, property, and name.

Sannyasin: A monk. One who has taken the vows of sannyasa, or renunciation.

Sat: Absolute, undifferentiated Existence. Also referred to as Infinite Being.

Sat-Chit-Ananda: Existence, Consciousness, and Bliss Absolute. According to the Vedanta philosophy, Sat-Chit-Ananda is the highest concept of God possible to the mind.

Sattva: One of the three primal qualities, or energies, that make up nature; Sattva is the quality of purity, goodness, and illumination. See *Gunas*.

Self: The same as Brahman, or the Infinite Spirit.

self: The ego, the small sense of "I."

Soham: Literally, "I am He." A mantra used by non-dualists to remind themselves that they are One with Brahman.

Soul: The same as Brahman, or the Infinite Spirit.

soul: The individual soul.

Sri: A prefix giving honor to the names of deities and eminent persons.

Swami: The title of a Hindu monk.

Tamas: One of the three primal qualities, or energies, that make up nature; Tamas is the quality of darkness, inertia, and ignorance. See *Gunas*.

Upanishads: The last revelations of the Vedas, where the Vedanta philosophy of Oneness is first and most beautifully proclaimed. There are 108 of them, of which eleven are called major Upanishads.

Vedanta: Literally, "the end," or "culmination," of the Vedas. A system of philosophy based upon the teachings of the Upanishads, proclaiming the final reality of Brahman, the One Existence, manifested as all things in the universe.

Vedas: The most sacred Hindu scriptures, consisting of four parts: the Rig, Sama, Yajur, and Atharva.

Viveka: Discrimination between the real and the unreal, between the One Infinite Existence and the temporary forms of the world.

Vritti: Literally, "whirlpool." A thought wave.

Yama: The first of the eight steps of Raja Yoga, made up of five restraints, or disciplines, that the devotee is called upon to practice and perfect.

Yoga: Union with God. Denotes the union of the individual soul with the Supreme Soul, and the disciplines that lead to such union. The four classical pathways to union with God are Bhakti, Jnana, Karma, and Raja.

Yogi: One who practices Yoga.

Bibliography

Books Recommended for Further Study:

Advaita Ashrama. *Vivekananda: A Biography in Pictures.* Calcutta: Advaita Ashrama, 1966.

Burke, Marie Louise. *Swami Vivekananda in the West: New Discoveries.* 3 vols. Calcutta: Advaita Ashrama, 1983–85.

Chetanananda, Swami, ed. *Vedanta: Voice of Freedom.* St. Louis: Vedanta Society of St. Louis, 1986.

His Eastern and Western Disciples. *The Life of Swami Vivekananda.* 2 vols. Calcutta: Advaita Ashrama, 1979–81.

Isherwood, Christopher. *Ramakrishna and His Disciples.* New York: Simon and Schuster, 1965.

Myren, Ann, and Dorothy Madison, eds. *Living at the Source.* Boston: Shambhala, 1993.

Nikhilananda, Swami, trans. *The Gospel of Sri Ramakrishna.* New York: Ramakrishna-Vivekananda Center, 1953.

———, ed. *Jnana Yoga.* New York: Ramakrishna-Vivekananda Center, 1955.

———, ed. *Karma Yoga and Bhakti Yoga.* New York: Ramakrishna-Vivekananda Center, 1955.

———, ed. *Raja Yoga.* New York: Ramakrishna-Vivekananda Center, 1956.

———. *Vivekananda: A Biography.* New York: Ramakrishna-Vivekananda Center, 1953.

————, ed. *Vivekananda: The Yogas and Other Works.* New York: Ramakrishna-Vivekananda Center, 1953.

Prabhavananda, Swami. *The Spiritual Heritage of India.* Hollywood: Vedanta Press, 1963.

Prabhavananda, Swami, and Christopher Isherwood, trans. *The Bhagavad-Gita: The Song of God.* Hollywood: Vedanta Press, 1951.

————, trans. *How to Know God: The Yoga Aphorisms of Patanjali.* Hollywood: Vedanta Press, 1966.

Prabhavananda, Swami, and Frederick Manchester, trans. *The Upanishads.* Hollywood: Vedanta Press, 1947.

Radhakrishnan, S. *Indian Philosophy.* 2 vols. New York: The Macmillan Co., 1923–27.

————, trans. *The Bhagavad Gita.* London: George Allen & Unwin Ltd., 1948.

Rolland, Romain. *The Life of Vivekananda and the Universal Gospel.* Calcutta: Advaita Ashrama, 1979.

Smith, Huston. *The World's Religions.* New York: Harper Collins, 1991.

Vivekananda, Swami. *The Complete Works of Swami Vivekananda.* 8 vols. Calcutta: Advaita Ashrama, 1962.

About the Editor

DAVE DELUCA has presented thousands of seminars, classes and trainings on all aspects of personal growth during his twenty years as a professional seminar leader. A long-time student of the ancient Vedanta wisdom of Oneness, he has been one of the West's most passionate and highly regarded Vedantic teachers for over a decade. He presented Vedanta at the *Parliament of the World's Religions* in Barcelona, Spain, and continues to give keynote addresses, classes and seminars on spiritual growth at conferences, churches, temples, learning centers, and retreats all over America and Canada.

To learn more about Dave and his work, please visit www.davedeluca.com. If you would like to have Dave speak or present one of his seminars to your group, please contact him at dave@davedeluca.com.